*The Legacy
of Horace M. Kallen*

Horace M. Kallen. *(Courtesy of the New School for Social Research.)*

The Legacy
of Horace M. Kallen

Edited by
Milton R. Konvitz

A Herzl Press Publication

Rutherford ● *Madison* ● *Teaneck*
Fairleigh Dickinson University Press
London and Toronto: Associated University Presses

Associated University Presses
440 Forsgate Drive
Cranbury, NJ 08512

Associated University Presses
25 Sicilian Avenue
London WC1A 2QH, England

Associated University Presses
2133 Royal Windsor Drive
Unit 1
Mississauga, Ontario
Canada L5J 1K5

Herzl Press
515 Park Ave.
New York, NY 10022

The paper used in this publication meets the
requirements of the American National Standard for
Permanence of Paper for Printed Library Materials Z39.48-1984.

Library of Congress Cataloging-in-Publication Data

The Legacy of Horace M. Kallen.

"A Herzl Press Publication."
Includes bibliographies.
1. Kallen, Horace Meyer, 1882–1974. 2. Philosophers
—United States—Biography. I. Kallen, Horace Meyer,
1882–1974. II. Konvitz, Milton Ridvas, 1908–
B945.K28L44 1987   191   85-46028
ISBN 0-8386-3291-2 (alk. paper)

Printed in the United States of America

The Legacy of Horace M. Kallen

is dedicated to the revered memory
of

SAMUEL ROSENTHAL

linked with Horace Kallen in a bond
of mutual respect and friendship

"Friends also follow the law of divine necessity;
they gravitate to each other,
and cannot do otherwise . . ."
—Ralph Waldo Emerson

Contents

Acknowledgments

Acknowledgments are due to the following copyright owners and publishers for permission to use copyrighted materials: *Jewish Social Studies* for the papers by Ronald Kronish and Elmer N. Lear; *Modern Judaism* for the papers by Lewis S. Feuer, Sidney Ratner, and the essay "H. M. Kallen and the Hebraic Idea" by Milton R. Konvitz; and the *American Jewish Year Book*, for the essay "Horace Meyer Kallen (1882–1974): In Praise of Hyphenation and Orchestration" (originally "Horace Meyer Kallen [1882–1974]: Philosopher of the Hebraic-American Idea" by Milton R. Konvitz).

Preface

In his last book—*Creativity, Imagination, Logic*—completed just before his ninetieth birthday, Horace Kallen wrote:

> If . . . we have been bound to our dead in friendship, or love . . . or the togetherness and teamplay of shared causes, no consolation quite consoles. In the topology of our lives a place has been emptied where this one, no one else, could fit; and our future must need continue this emptiness and the hurt of it, strive as we may to fill it. We live on, perhaps even more abundantly than before our loss, nevertheless with that singularity missed, a note in the orchestration of our selfhood silenced, and the silence not a rest but a break. Indeed, it may happen that the silence turns intolerable, however it may be compensated with the ongoing validities of survival. We need our dead alive, somehow. . . . [D]eath is simply an instant nothingness . . . between living on where we are now and living on hereafter in an Afterworld. (P. 198)

When Kallen wrote that, he had in mind his own need to have somehow alive the many dead to whom he was bound in love, or friendship, or the togetherness of shared interests and loyalties, who were part of his Afterworld. We are the Afterworld in which Horace Kallen lives.

But the Afterworld that we now provide will in time be filled by others than ourselves, and they, too, will provide for Kallen honorable and significant place, for Kallen has left the world rich intellectual and moral legacy that will survive as long as humanity will strive to give meaning to the ideals that alone make life worth living.

Until his death in 1974 at the age of ninety-one, Kallen was esteemed as one of America's leading social philosophers, and his death has not eclipsed his reputation. For over fifty years his name had been intimately associated with the New School for Social Research, whose original distinguished faculty he had joined in 1919. He was a pioneer in introducing Zionism in the United States and had worked closely with Justice Brandeis and Judge Julian

Mack in the reorganization of the American Zionist movement. He was one of the founders of the American Jewish Congress, and of the American Association for Jewish Education (since 1981 known as the Jewish Education Service of North America). He was prominently identified with work on behalf of consumerism long before there was any public interest in the subject. He was active in civil rights and civil liberties organizations, in adult education, and in the building of cultural and educational institutions in Israel. Many interests, many causes found a congenial place in Kallen's wide-ranging, insatiable mind.

To celebrate the centenary of his birth (11 August 1882), a one-day conference was arranged by the New School for Social Research, the American Jewish Congress, and the American Section of the World Jewish Congress—institutions with which Kallen's life had been intimately intertwined. Three of the essays included in the present volume were originally presented at the centennial conference, which was held at the New School on 13 October 1982. These three essays are joined by four other papers, all of them selected because they discuss the major themes of Kallen's work and interests. In such discussion it is inevitable that there be some overlap and repetition, but in a composite book in which six scholars concentrate on the work of one philosopher, the repetition has the virtue of emphasizing the most significant aspects of the legacy of Horace Kallen.

I wish to thank Dr. Jacob Katzman and Professor Monty N. Penkower for their contributions to the success of the centennial conference.

I wish to thank, too, Leighton R. Rosenthal and Charlotte R. Kramer—the son and daughter of Professor Kallen's, as well as my own, dear friend, the late Samuel Rosenthal—who are trustees of the Samuel Rosenthal Foundation, which has made publication of this volume possible.

M. R. K.

Horace Meyer Kallen (1882–1974)
In Praise of Hyphenation and Orchestration

MILTON R. KONVITZ

Several months before his death on 16 February 1974, at the age of ninety-one, Horace Kallen saw the publication of his latest book, *Creativity, Imagination, Logic,* and had begun to write another. In the same few months, he conducted a seminar in consumerism and cooperatives at the New School for Social Research, where he had taught since 1919 and was the last surviving member of the original faculty, which had included Charles Beard, John Dewey, and Alvin Johnson. Also in those same few months, he wrote a pamphlet, *Consumerism, Cooperatism and the Idea of the Consumer,* that was published jointly by the Rochdale Institute, of which Kallen was a founder and a trustee, and the New School; and the University Press of Virginia published his pamphlet, *Toward a Philosophy of the Seas,* in which was included his essay, "The Humanities of the Sea and the Future of Mankind," that he had delivered in 1972 as a lecture at the University of Virginia.

These facts are cited to convey Kallen's remarkable energy and stamina, his wide-ranging interests, his dedication to the life of the intellect and spirit, his eagerness to grapple with new problems and to test himself against new challenges. The value of a man's life, Montaigne observed, lies not in the length of days, but in the use he makes of them. In the case of Horace Kallen, we see the fortunate conjuncture of a long and a useful life; for he lived his days with the desperate eagerness of a man destined to die young—as if he had been marked for death, like Pascal, at thirty-nine, or Spinoza, at forty-five. Although aware of some external marks of aging, he felt sound and youthful, and when the end came, he was in a restaurant with his wife and some friends: there was no struggle with the enemy, no pain, "no sadness of

15

farewell," no "lonely spasm of helpless agony"—it was a death he passionately must have wished for, almost as if he had invited it, as Socrates had in
his prison cell in Athens. A man needs to be fortunate in dying, as in living.

Horace Kallen was blessed with a strong physique, a vigor of body and
mind, a presence that marked him to strangers and friends alike as a special
person, as the embodiment of qualities that identified him as a man who
surely was famous; as someone who must be a celebrity; as someone who had
position, titles, and honors. He had what is best expressed by the Hebrew
phrase, *hadrat panim*, the beauty of physical presence that expressed the
qualities of greatness of mind and soul.

His Life

Horace Kallen was born on 11 August 1882, in Berenstadt, a town in the
German province of Silesia (now Poland).[1] His father, Jacob David, came to
Germany from Latvia, had studied at a *yeshivah*, and could have been a
hazzan, a *shohet*, and a *mohel;* he functioned as Berenstadt's assistant rabbi.
Horace Kallen remembered his father as he was years later, a man with a long
white beard, glittering blue eyes, both friendly and intimidating. He was
expelled from Germany as a foreigner and made his way to the United States.
When Horace was about five years old, his father returned to Berenstadt to
move his wife, Esther Rebecca; Horace, who was the eldest child; and his two
daughters to the United States, where he became rabbi of the German-
speaking Orthodox congregation Hevra ha-Moriah in Boston.

Rabbi Jacob David Kallen (originally Kalonymus, the name of many
medieval Jewish families, including one of the most distinguished in Germany from the ninth to the thirteenth centuries) was a scholarly man. At the
time of his death in 1917, he left some manuscripts that remain unpublished.
While Horace Kallen felt close to his mother (she died in 1928), he was
alienated from his father, whom he remembered as a proud, demanding,
domineering father and husband. For many years they were not on speaking
terms (in such cases we usually have only the son's version; it would be
interesting and instructive to have also the father's side of the story). When his
father was on his deathbed, Horace was summoned, and he remained with
him for about two weeks, until he died. In that fortnight, father and son—
Kallen said many years later—reached "a sort of reciprocal respect and, to
some degree, understanding." In his study at home, Professor Kallen had on
his wall framed photographs of both his father and his mother.

Kallen did not start to attend elementary school until he was eight or nine,
when the truant officer threatened his father. The boy was taught at home by
his father and also attended Hebrew schools; and to help maintain the
growing family (eventually there were eight children), he sold newspapers—

over the proud father's strong objections. Rabbi Kallen wanted his son to follow in his footsteps, but Horace rebelled and at times ran away from home. His memories of those dismal years—the period that saw him through *heder* and elementary and secondary schools—troubled him for the remainder of his life. The deathbed reconciliation with his father did not engage his heart; he did not sit *shivah* nor recite the *kaddish* for his father, and whenever he spoke of him, he found it hard not to interject a harsh word.

When he was eighteen, Kallen entered Harvard College and after three years, in 1903, received the B.A. degree *magna cum laude*. For his intellectual and spiritual development, these were perhaps the most important years of his life. His interest in philosophy, however, began only shortly before he left for Harvard, when he was still living at home and discovered among his father's books a copy of Spinoza's *Ethics* and *Tractatus Theologico-Politicus* in German translations. These were quite enough to excite his youthful, eager mind. Then, as a freshman at Harvard, he took a philosophy course with Santayana and, in the following year, with William James, on whom he thereafter looked as his master.

At this time he knew, of course, that he was excluded from Christian society, and he intentionally separated himself from his Jewish background and heritage. But in his sophomore year, when he was being so strongly influenced and motivated by William James, he took a course in American literary history with Barrett Wendell, whose teaching attempted to articulate the Hebraic elements in American political and literary thought and institutions. Kallen tried to resist and reject Wendell's teaching but, in private conferences with his argumentative student, Wendell won out, and Kallen then began consciously and conscientiously to reclaim, and to identify himself with, his Jewish inheritance, Jewish culture, and the Jewish community. It was not that he accepted from Professor Wendell what he had rejected from Rabbi Kallen. He maintained throughout his life a strong anticlerical suspicion and bias: he rejected Judaism insofar as it is a religion; his anticlericalism and agnosticism became transmuted into Jewish secularism, Jewish culture, Zionism, Hebraism, and cultural pluralism.

After graduating from Harvard, Kallen took a position at Princeton as an instructor in English. He remained there for two years (1903–05); his contract was not renewed. It was intimated that had the administration known that he was a Jew, he would not have been appointed in the first place. It was also suggested that he was undesirable because he taught atheism. When he discussed this incident in his old age, Kallen rhetorically asked how one could teach Shelley without talking about atheism. (Later, Ludwig Lewisohn wrote in *Upstream* about the difficulties encountered by a Jew who wanted to teach English literature.)

Kallen returned to Harvard as a graduate student. While at Princeton, he had thought he would write his doctoral dissertation on John Marston, the seventeenth-century English satirist and dramatist; but when he came back to Harvard, he resumed his philosophical studies, wrote his dissertation under James's direction on the nature of truth, and received his Ph.D. degree in 1908. For the next three years he was a lecturer at Harvard and assistant to James, Santayana, and Josiah Royce, the three philosophical giants who made Harvard preeminent and gave it a worldwide reputation. For one semester in this period Kallen was an instructor in logic at Clark. In 1907, before he completed his graduate studies, he received a Sheldon fellowship that made it possible for him to go to Europe to study with the noted pragmatist philosopher F. C. S. Schiller at Oxford, and to attend the lectures of Henri Bergson in Paris. James sent Kallen $250, insisting that these were royalties on one of his books, which he wanted Kallen to have; and Wendell wrote offering to lend him money. Before Kallen's return, Wendell set up for him at Harvard a course in aesthetics, which he could give that summer.

In 1911 Kallen became an instructor in philosophy and psychology at the University of Wisconsin, where he remained until 1918. He resigned from his position over issues of academic freedom: his English friend Norman Angell, author of *The Great Illusion* (1910), who later was knighted and received the Nobel Peace Prize, was denied the right to speak on the campus because of his seemingly pacifist views. The faculty also sought to win unanimous approval from its members for a statement condemning United States Senator Robert M. LaFollette for his antiwar position. Kallen felt that he differed with the faculty over fundamental questions of academic freedom; that the academic atmosphere of the campus had been seriously compromised by intolerance and politics.

But his years at Wisconsin were productive ones, for it was in those years that he published *William James and Henri Bergson: A Study in Contrasting Theories of Life* (1914), *The Structure of Lasting Peace* (1918), and *The Book of Job as a Greek Tragedy* (1918). In that period, too, *The Nation* published his articles containing the first formulation of his philosophy of cultural pluralism (1915). And it was in those years that he became deeply involved in Zionist thought and action. Had he been judged by the test of "publish or perish!" he would have been given tenure and a professorship, and other inducements to remain. But Kallen was restless; he wanted very much to be in Boston or New York, where he could attend meetings—especially Zionist meetings—and influence men and action. Accordingly, when he received an invitation in 1919 to join Thorstein Veblen, James Harvey Robinson, and other famous scholars who comprised the original faculty of the New School for Social Research, he accepted and remained there to teach for over half a century.

But Kallen was never the typical professional or careerist philosopher. This is how he saw himself in 1935:

Although I feel philosophy as a calling and enjoy teaching it, I have not been able to devote myself exclusively to what is euphemistically known as "scholarship" and the sheer academic life. My earliest interests were as literary as philosophical, and were soon crossed by direct participation in political and economic movements of the land, especially those aiming at the protection and growth of freedom, including the labor movement, the civil liberties union and the consumers' cooperative movement. Hence I have never attained that fullness of pedagogical withdrawal which custom and prejudice ordain for the practice of philosophy in America. Unable to separate my profession from my life, I have always found myself ill at ease with the philosophy and the psychology of the schools. The first has seemed to me for the most part a ceremonial liturgy of professionals as artificial and detached from the realities of the daily life as bridge or chess or any other safe but exciting game of chance, and much of the second has seemed to me the sedulous elaboration of disregard for the living man of flesh and blood.[2]

When he considered the philosophic disciplines in the mid-1950s, he saw them "as heroic endeavors after a precision denied by their own history and by the nature of things. They are, like all their kind, sisyphean labors. . . . What I deprecate in them is a certain self-isolation, a cultivated tangency and irrelevancy to the rest of the human enterprise."

Who were the men who influenced Kallen? In 1935 he wrote that the "paramount influences" on the development of his attitude, point of view, and method were William James, George Santayana, Barrett Wendell, F. C. S. Schiller, Edwin B. Holt, and Solomon Schechter. In later years he added John Dewey, and at times mentioned also Justice Louis D. Brandeis and Edward Everett Hale, famous Boston Unitarian minister, reformer, and author. Among the pictures on the walls of his study, first in New York and then in Oneonta, were portraits of Jefferson, Goethe, James, Santayana, Hale, Dewey, Judge Julian Mack, and Schechter—it was for them—and Wendell—that he reserved a lasting pious and affectionate reverence. Only his spirit and heart could have tied together their diverse natures into a confraternity of intimate friends.

And only his spirit and mind could have tied together—or orchestrated, as he liked to put it—such a multiplicity of diverse interests as adult education, worker education, Jewish education, general education, consumerism, the labor movement, the cooperative movement, Zionism, art and aesthetics, censorship and civil liberties, the philosophy of secular Judaism, the Book of Job, the League of Nations and the United Nations, civil rights, pragmatism, the philosophy of pluralism, the philosophy of individualism, the nature of comedy, the State of Israel, and the whole of Western, especially American, culture and civilization. The institutions Kallen helped found or supported to his last day—the American Jewish Congress, the American Association for Jewish Education, the New School for Social Research, the Rochdale Institute, the Jewish Teachers Seminary–Herzliah, the Farband, and the Labor Zionist Alliance—were treasures for him, and this showed where his heart lay.[3]

Individualism

Kallen at different times gave different names to that of which we now think as his intellectual and moral legacy. The name depended on what he wished to emphasize at the time. He called his philosophy scientific humanism, free humanism, aesthetic pragmatism, cultural pluralism, individualism, the American Idea, Hebraisim; but I doubt if he was pleased with any label, for he had a deep dread of all *isms*, all ideologies—anything that suggested a closed body of thought, a system of neatly organized propositions. This is one reason why he could not think of himself as a professional philosopher, for as we have seen, he could not separate his profession from his life, nor play with thought as something artificial and detached from the realities of daily life. His thoughts had to be part of an ongoing process, just as his life was. And his life had to be open to whatever it would bring from without or within, and had to be open to welcome the unforeseen and the unforseeable. If, as the Talmud suggest, fifty gates of understanding had been created in the world, Kallen would have liked to believe that all of them were turned over to him. Given such total openness to life, experience, and truth; and given the belief that the intellect is not the only instrument of knowing, but that one can also know through joy, love, the physical senses, even through dancing and singing, how then can one have a clearly defined system of thought?

And yet Horace Kallen's work does show a configuration, a unity, that can be described and discussed. When Kallen finished his last book and came to writing its introduction, he said that, as he read the whole, he found to his surprise that the book had an "unexpected continuity." He wrote:

> I do experience a unity, not the structured unity built by the logic of a systematic treatise but the unity of intermittent unification generated by the confluence, next to next, of waves of consciousness.[4]

When one reads Kallen's major works, one finds, I would say, an even greater degree of unity. They show more than a succession of waves of consciousness. He had a certain way of looking at the world and at life. His mind kept returning to certain themes. He had his affirmations and his negations, his affinities and rejections, his loyalties and hatreds. He did not want to feel that this thought was arrested at any one point: he wanted to feel and believe that his thought was arrested at any one point: he wanted to feel and believe that strange adventures and encounters were just over the line he had reached and were there waiting for his pushing and probing, that his writing was as much exploration as it was recording. But no man can stand on tiptoe very long. Balboa discovered the Pacific only once. The greatest philosophers, Plato and Kant, for example, had eseentially one or two ideas that they spent their lifetimes developing, testing, modifying, applying, explaining.

If, as Kallen has said, William James was the first democrat in meta-physics,[5] then Horace Kallen, we may add, was the second. Both James and Kallen broke with a long philosophic tradition that can be traced back to the pre-Socratic Greeks and from them to Kant and Hegel, F. H. Bradley, and Josiah Royce. That tradition accepted as a fundamental premise a radical distinction between appearance and reality. Time, space, motion, and be-coming, the world as experienced by the senses—to quote Bishop Berkeley, all the "furniture of earth—in a word, all those bodies which compose the mighty frame of the world"—were somehow not quite real and belonged to the world of appearance.

James and Kallen refused to accept the distinction between appearance and reality as aboriginal and final. To them, the distinction was secondary and functional.[6] They looked for nature and reality, not in abstractions and logical processes but in the data of experience and the insights offered by the intelligence. They did not try to build systems, but looked for instruction in the piecemeal character of knowledge and the plural character of reality that this knowledge disclosed and apprehended. In the place of a universe, they found a multiverse; in the place of one order, they found either no order at all or many orders, perhaps an infinity of orders, all of equal reality and value. In the place of a single whole, single neatly organized system or Absolute, James and Kallen found variety and multitudinousness of experience. Instead of denying appearance as error or illusion, they affirmed the reality of identity and change, of continuation and mutation, of the confluence of past and future.[7] They affirmed the reality of "real duration," of "process," of becoming, change, and novelty. They rejected rigid materialism and mecha-nistic explanations and accepted the possibility of chance and uniqueness, the reality of surprise and contingency.[8]

In brief, in his metaphysics Kallen, like James, was a pluralist and a temporalist. He rejected as invidious any sharp distinction between ap-pearance and reality. He was concerned with consequences and not with freezing essences or hypostatizing ideas or ideals. He held that percepts were basic and that concepts were secondary and derivative. There are unities as well as parts, but unities are important only as instrumental. There are relations but they are external and only associative. There are no finalities, no foregone conclusions, no certainties, no guarantees.[9]

The metaphysical pluralism that was James's became the cultural pluralism of Kallen. Cotton Mather, Kallen wrote, came to fruition in Channing, and Jonathan Edwards came to fruition in Emerson.[10] In the same spirit we can say that William James came to fruition in Horace Kallen. To see them in this relationship is not to detract value or dignity from either, but rather to add to the originality and worth of each.

Applying pluralism to the human scene, Kallen disavowed the state or society as the social absolute. If there are any absolutes, there are many—as many as there are individuals, for individuals are the human pluriverse. They are the primary data and the primary values, and all principalities and powers, all societies and states, all kingdoms and governments are derivative and secondary. Men stand in relation to one another, but the relations are external ones. Society or the state is not an organic entity, but an association of men who are free to disassociate and to form new societies, new states, and new governments.

In his belief in the primacy of the individual Kallen went beyond James and John Dewey, and, in this respect, we can associate his radical thought only with Jefferson and Emerson.

No thinker since John Locke, in his *Second Treatise of Civil Government*, put the case of individualism in stronger terms. Kallen wrote in 1933:

> As a matter of scientific fact, individuals and societies are incommensurable assemblies. Analogies from one to the other are drawn at the drawer's own risk. No earthly society has ever been an organism. Many or few individuals have composed each, entering it, leaving it, working for it or against it, as the occasion indicated; and when need was, destroying it and organizing themselves into a new society.
>
> States, churches, industries, families are organizations, not organisms. They are associations of men and women occurring not because they inwardly must, but because an outward condition calls for control or manipulation which individuals cannot accomplish alone. There are no social institutions which are primary, which are ends in themselves and to themselves, as individuals are ends to and in themselves.[11]

Almost a quarter of a century later, Kallen wrote: "I believe in the primacy of the individual because I can find no other human seat than individuality for choice, for decision, for the initiation of action."[12] The elemental term in every union, every association is "the individual in his indefeasible singularity."[13] The American Idea starts with the individual; society and government, if they are to be justified, must be justified in his eyes and by his instincts; hence, all association is voluntary.[14] Kallen stated:

> Society is indeed only the name for the endlessly varying ways in which individuals associate with one another. Whatever a man's faith and loyalty, however mean and slavish his life, narrow his aspirations and limited his choices, to himself he counts as uniquely one; to his companions, his friends, his enemies, his masters or his underlings, he may not count uniquely, but he counts still as one. In his very submissiveness and acquiescence there is a core of choice, a unique and personal rejection of the burdens of freedom, the dangers of defiance, of conflict and self-assertion, an exhibition, therefore, of individuality.[15]

However, the name and fame of Horace Kallen are identified with the idea of culture and with the philosophy of cultural pluralism, and these ideas imply the concept of *group* existence, of identification of the individual with a group and its customs, laws, loyalties, and ideals. How, then, did Kallen come to connect the individual with group life and group functions?

Cultural Pluralism

Part of the answer to this question is to be found in Kallen's biography. As we have seen, by the time he reached Harvard at the age of eighteen, Horace Kallen's feelings toward Judaism were not only negative but hostile; he thought of Jewishness as an affliction that an enlightened person should seek to discard. But Barrett Wendell, a Christian, "converted" Kallen to Judaism. He did not return to his father or to his father's religion, but to the Jewish heritage of culture, thought, and values, to the feeling of membership in the Jewish people, to a lively sensitivity to the Jewish being and the Jewish experience. Like Heine, Kallen felt as if he had never really left Judaism and the Jewish community, and the "conversion" was only a restoration of his sight.

Before long, Kallen discovered Zionism and threw himself into Zionist work.[16] In 1902 Solomon Schechter came to the United States to become head of the Jewish Theological Seminary, and soon thereafter young Horace Kallen came to think of him as his "revered friend and teacher."[17] When Kallen received his B.A. degree, all the essential components of his philosophy of cultural pluralism were already parts of his intellectual, moral, and spiritual equipment. All that he needed was the formula that would instruct him on the mixing process, and this he discovered and made public in his historically important articles in *The Nation*.[18] Years later, Kallen himself stated what had come to pass:

> . . . the commingling of James's lectures and Wendell's [literary history] crystallized in my mind into a new outlook, the results of which were: first, discovery of the meaning of "equal" as used in the Declaration [of Independence]; second, recognition of the social role of freedom and of individual and group differences, later to be expounded at length in my own philosophy, and finally, such a reappraisal of my Jewish affiliations as required an acquiescence in my Jewish inheritance and heritage, an expanding exploration into the content and history of both, and a progressively greater participation in Jewish communal enterprises.[19]

What was true of Jewish difference, he knew, was true as well of all other ethnic-cultural groupings, "each with its own singularity of form and utterance."[20]

In his first formulation of cultural pluralism,[21] Kallen thought only of the ethnic groups to which Americans belonged, and he thought of membership in the group as something the individual could not easily shed. An association

was either natural or voluntary, either a *Gemeinschaft* or a *Gesellschaft;*[22] the
ethnic group was the former, a natural community. "Jews or Poles or Anglo-
Saxons," wrote Kallen in 1915, "in order to cease being Jews or Poles or
Anglo-Saxons would have to cease to be, while they could cease to be citizens
or church members or carpenters or lawyers without ceasing to be."[23] A
man, he said, cannot change his grandfather.[24]

Later, while continuing to believe that participation in one's ethnic group
and its special, unique culture had great significance for a person's self-
identification, sense of dignity and worth, and for his full development,
Kallen tended to think that, without exception, all associations were, or
ought to be, voluntary; for a person has the liberty to reject the fact that he is
a Jew or a Pole or an Anglo-Saxon; a man cannot change, but he can reject his
grandfather, as indeed many men have done. In a free society, membership in
a group is effected not by status but by contract.[25]

From the very beginning, Kallen's individualism was not solipsistic. No
individual, he wrote, is merely an individual;[26] the elemental term in every
group or association or union of persons, he always urged, is "the individual
in his indefeasible singularity." But, he hastily added, "I know of no instance
. . . of an individual building his personal history solely by himself, from
himself, on himself; feeding, so to speak, on nothing but his own flesh and
spirit and growing by what he feeds on."[27] According to Kallen, "rugged
individualism" can be viewed only as a case of extreme selfishness; when
invoked as an ideal, it is only used to defeat individuality. Inherent in
individualsim, as understood by Kallen, is the principle of cooperation, but
cooperation that is voluntary, that does not replace the primacy of the
individual with the primacy of a society based on the principle of the organic
interdependence of men.[28]

How Horace Kallen wove together the different strands of thought, with
the skill and delicate hand of a master, cannot be explained; it can only be
illustrated by his own writings. The following passage is typical:

> Drag or push and pull, each society is, for the individuals in whose lives it
> lives, a patterned environment. Its formations so work as to strengthen and
> enlarge, or to weaken and contract, his personal singularity. . . . The more
> of them [societies] he can join or leave, the more varied their forms and
> functions, the more abundant, the freer, the richer, the more civilized, is
> likely to be the personality which lives and moves and nourishes its being
> among the diverse communions. It is the variety and range of his participa-
> tion which does in fact distinguish a civilized man from an uncivilized, a
> man of faith and reason from an unreasoning fanatic, a democrat from a
> totalitarian, a man of culture from a barbarian. Such a man obviously
> orchestrates a growing pluralism of associations into the wholeness of his
> individuality.[29]

Who among those who have known Horace Kallen can fail to see in these
words a self-portrait, no less than a summary of his essential position as a

temporalist, an instrumentalist, a pragmatist, a humanist, an American, a Jew, and a hundred and one other things that he was? "The hyphen," he wrote, "unites very much more than it separates."[30] He was, without doubt, the most hyphenated American thinker, and so lived more abundantly, more freely, more richly, and to whomever and to whatever he was united, he gave more abundantly, more freely, more richly.

Education of Free Men

Horace Kallen shared with Locke and Jefferson the belief that all men have inherent and inalienable rights, and the right to, and capacity for, self-government. Kallen thought in terms of the primacy of the individual and his inherent and inalienable rights, a primacy that must not be compromised by, or shared with, culture, society, state, or government. These rights, together with self-government, imply or define equality and freedom.

Kallen never tired of articulating these basic assumptions and their implications for social organization, for educational philosophy and practice, and for Jewish education and culture.[31] He saw human rights as inherent in, or constitutive of, the nature of each human being. Therefore, they derive from his nature, and not from any document, constitution, or contract. For bills of rights are themselves derivative: they do not give, but only profess or proclaim rights inherent in individuals—rights from which no individual may be alienated without compromise of his human nature.

Given inherent and inalienable rights and the capacity for, and right to, self-government, equality and freedom are inevitable marks of man and the societies of men. The equal exercise of these rights leads to diversity among men and their societies; and what is equality, asks Kallen, if it is not the right to be different? In a democracy men are unavoidably different because each expresses his inherent nature and exercises his right to self-government according to his inherent nature. This is why mere toleration is repugnant to the democratic position. For democracy, "difference, otherness, is not the same as wrong and evil; the unlike is eqully good and right *as* unlike and *because* unlike."

So, too, men are unavoidably free if each expresses his inherent nature and exercises his right to self-government. Freedom, in Kallen's philosophy, is inseparable from human nature; it is not a mere means, but an aim or end, and the uses of freedom are a means to freedom.

Is a society of self-governing, free and freedom-loving, equal and different individuals an anarchic one? Not at all. "In so far as it is a society of friends," says Kallen, "it is an orderly society." By the process of orchestration, "the unique and the diverse in being and spirit" are brought "to mutual appreciation and respect, to pleasure in one another, to cooperation with one another, or at worst to agreeing to disagree." The "union of the different" constitutes the spirit of the society or nation, or association of nations. "It is sustained, not by mutual exclusions, nor by the rule of one over others, but by their equality and by the free trade between these different equals in every good thing the community's life and culture produce." The free exchange of thoughts and things among the different who are equal leads to forging bonds, the hyphenation which is "a bridge from each to each and all to all."

The implications of this philosophy for democratic education—education for free men—are clear enough; for, "Education is civilization and civilization is hyphenation."

Not long ago, a leader of the Zionist movement spoke disparagingly of "hyphenated Jews," maintaining that in Israel Jews can be Jews without hyphenation. The answer to him is to be found in Kallen's books. "A society's existence is strengthened," says Kallen, "its life is enriched, in the degree that its members may pass unhindered from it to any other, making free exchange of the thoughts and things of each, in the degree that the members are hyphenated, and the hyphen is a bond of union, a bridge from each to each and all to all."

Hyphenation, or cultural pluralism, is made possible by education; education makes possible "freedom and fellowship of different people *as* different." Education makes possible the justification of self-government, "sustaining and enlarging the equal rights of different human beings diversely to live and to grow in liberty and happiness." For the task of education is "overcoming the isolations of spirit and flesh which tradition sustains; generating, by means of the arts and sciences of free communication, mutuality of respect, understanding and sympathy among the different cultures of our civilization; initiating such a habit of team play with the different that every people, every culture, every individual of every people and culture, experiences a greater fulfillment in freedom than by struggling on alone." The education of free men makes possible "a union of the different on equal terms," which is identical with hyphenation. Hyphenation and orchestration are thus two sides of the same coin. Implied in these concepts are the basic assumptions of democracy: equality and freedom, inherent and inalienable rights of individuals, the right to and capacity for self-government. And the philosophy and program of liberal education imply the basic assumptions of democracy, and are implicit in these assumptions.[32]

It is thus clear that education and democracy are interdependent. In a letter to Jarvis in 1820, Jefferson wrote: "I know no safe depository of the ultimate powers of society but the people themselves; and if we think them not enlightened enough to exercise their control with a wholesome discretion, the remedy is not to take it from them, but to inform discretion by education. This is the true corrective of abuses of political power." In a letter to Yancey in 1816, Jefferson wrote: "If a nation expects to be ignorant and free in a state of civilization, it expects what never was and never shall be." Freedom may be an individual's inalienable right, but the security of this right, says Kallen, lies in knowledge.

The education with which democracy is inextricably connected is obviously not to be identified with teaching that is the mere transmission of a permanent body of facts or beliefs. Its aim is rather to conserve and nourish the power to learn, "that is, to change and grow," to appraise and change the past "toward ever greater freedom and friendship of people, whatever their origins, status, faith, sex or occupation."

The belief in inherent and inalienable rights does not assume a human nature that is fixed, a mental or spiritual endowment that is beyond education. On the contrary, democracy implies that "human traits can be made." Democracy rejects "invariant" personality in favor of "changing" personality. But the individual plays a role "in his own making." The idea that one's heredity or environment is a factor external to the person leaves no room, says Kallen, "for the most intimate and the most lasting of Everyman's experiences—the experience that he is, even at his most passive, diversely up and doing, selecting, rejecting, excreting, assimilating, from among the multitudinous alternatives which present themselves for his response, those that then and there engage and enchannel his powers most livingly and variedly." Kallen agrees with Pascal that "there is nothing which he [man] may not make natural; there is nothing natural which he may not lose."[33]

Thus even inherent and inalienable rights need protection against loss and alienation, and their protection is one of the tasks of democratic education. It has always been to the merit of Jeffersonian believers in inherent and inalienable rights that they have not relied on the inherent and inalienable character of individual rights for their preservation. On the contrary, they have always been foremost proponents of universal and free education, of the system of checks and balances, and of written constitutions and bills of rights, and believers in the interdependence of force and freedom. Knowing that inherent rights can be lost and that inalienable rights can be alienated, Jeffersonian democrats have ever been ready to fight to win, maintain, or enlarge their liberties. Says Kallen:

> Such is the free man, inwardly at least, the master of his fate, the captain of his soul, the man who has chosen his destiny, who has held fast to his difference, his individuality, and not yielded. His faith in his choice is the efficacious energy of his power not to yield. His choosing is a condition of active tension, of holding his own without any assurance that the rest of the world will cooperate, with the future open and unguaranteed.

Thus the free man takes his stand for hyphenation and seeks the orchestration of differences among equals. He will strive for orchestration even if his very life be at stake; and he will strive for the right to be different, to be hyphenated in his own fashion, and according to his own bent, even if his very life be at stake. The free man is a citizen of an open city. The defense of his city always depends on him. Every minute of his life he is existentially involved in his freedom and citizenship. Hyphenation equally guarantees war and peace; for orchestration, like freedom, is never given, but must be taken.

Inherent in hyphenation and orchestration is the commitment to seek peace, to live and let live. But the commitment to hyphenation and orchestration is challenged by the absolutist and totalitarian, all those who insist that one can live on their terms only. Antihyphenation is committed to aggression, to live but not to let live. Therefore, lasting peace requires education for peace: education of free men for a free world.

Professor Kallen's philosophy of education grows intimately out of his assumptions regarding the nature and political theory of man. His system of thought was carefully and adequately articulated as he struggled at various times with the central problems of psychology, aesthetics, science, religion, politics, Zionism, literature, education, and morals.

The Greeks, said Kallen, sought structure, harmony, immutable and eternal order. The Jew, on the other hand, saw the world as in flux, and events occurring according to no predetermined plan. In the Hebraic view, he held,

> Sin got its punishment, virtue its rewards. But no man was immutably sinful, no divine fiat eternal and unalterable. There is room for atonement, for a readjustment and a new life. . . . The thing is exemplified best in the greater tragedies, which portray the inexorable working of ancestral curse. Destiny is necessary. For the Hebrew, an alteration of life means an *alteration of destiny.* A "repentant" man means a "forgiving" God. In a word, for the Greeks, change is unreal and evil; for the Hebrews the essence of reality is change. The Greek view of reality is static and structural; the Hebrew view is dynamic and functional.[34]

When science is viewed from the Greek point of view, said Kallen, the subject of research has to be seen as "eternal and immutable substance, as forms, genera, species, varieties, existing eternally in their Aristotelian classifications." Darwin's theory, however, with its principles of spontaneous generation and the survival of the fit, dealt a deathblow to scientific Hellenism. The Darwinian approach is "to espouse the flux, to allow for the reality of individuals as against classes, to allow for genuine freedom and chance in the world, to insist on the concrete instance rather than on the general law—in a word," Kallen concluded, "to give an overwhelming scientific background to the Hebraic as against the Hellenic visions of the nature of reality."[35]

Kallen found the Hebraic view of reality and the Hebraic ways of thought in Darwin and in the epistemological and ethical aspects of William James's philosophy; he found them, too, in the metaphysical views of Henri Bergson. For Bergson, wrote Kallen, the structure of things is only an incident, "a mere instant or position through which the *life* of the world passes. Change and not immutability is found real; the static and not the dynamic is found to be 'mere appearance,' unreal." And Kallen adds: "But such a finding is the essential finding of Hebraism. In philosophic thought, it is exceedingly recent, but promises to be philsophically dominant." He concluded that, through the work of James and Bergson, the metaphysic of Hebraism opened a new era in the history of philosophy, in which Hellenism will be subordinated to Hebraism.

Believing that thought is a prelude to action, Horace Kallen translated his Hebraic thought into Zionist action. In an article published in 1910, Kallen proclaimed, "I am a Zionist," and proceeded to explain: "I look toward the concentration and renationalization of the Jews. I am committed to the persistence of a 'Jewish separation' that shall be national, positive, dynamic and adequate."[36]

As noted before, Kallen found that in metaphysics the historic content of Hebraism was the vision of reality in flux. He discovered that, in morals, the Hebraic conception centered on the value of the individual; and in the Hebraic religion, the central stress was on God as the moral arbiter who commanded a life of righteousness. But throughout history Hebraism found its sustenance and security in the life of the group, the ethnic group known as the Hebraic or Jewish people. They were Jews, not merely Judaists. "What really destroys the Jews," wrote Kallen in 1910, "is what 'universalizes' them, what empties their life of distinctive particular content and substitutes void phrases to be filled with any meaning the social and religious fashion of the day casts up. Hebraism, what 'Israel has stood for in history,' is the life of the Jews, their unique achievement—not as isolated individuals, but as a well-defined ethnic group—in government, in industry and commerce, in social economy, in the arts, in religion, in philosophy." The historic personality of the Jewish people, he wrote in 1916, is "that social and spiritual complex of group qualities and customs which constitute nationality." And he added, "Today in the modern, democratic world, the integrating force which articulates nationality is Zionism."[37]

In 1919 Kallen argued that democracy is antiassimilationist. Democracy "stands for the acknowledgment, the harmony and organization of group diversities in cooperative expansion of the common life, not for the assimilation of diversities into sameness. Zionism is antiassimilationist because it is democratic, because it has enough faith . . . to apply its teachings to groups as well as to individuals."[38] With Mazzini, Kallen saw democracy and nationalism joined together in the struggle against oppression, and he offered as summary of Mazzini's teaching an adaptation of the Declaration of Independence: that all nationalities are created equal and endowed with certain inalienable rights, and that among these are life, liberty, and the pursuit of happiness. And, Kallen added, "This is the whole Zionist ideology."

It was within the context of his concern with Hebraism and Zionism that

Kallen argued that, from the eighteenth century on, liberalism overplayed the idea of the isolated individual. It failed to see that individuality does not come with birth but is achieved, and that all men depend in their beginning on a society which is a *natio* before it is anything else. Genuine liberalism, he continued, requires for the group, for races, or nationalities, "the same freedom of development and expression as for the individual." Indeed, "in requiring it for the individual, it must necessarily require it for them. They [that is, nations and races] are the essential reservoirs of individuality."

Through national freedom, the Jewish people would be in a position to render service to mankind. Its aim to achieve the liberation of the Jewish people and the reconstitution of their national home, made Zionism a part of the tradition and aspiration of democracy. Zionism, Kallen wrote, "conceives human society as a democratic cooperative organization of nationalities, no less than of other forms of the associations of men in the endeavor after life, liberty and happiness, and it claims for the Jews opportunity and security in this type of association." For the Jew will not win his emancipation as a human being, as an individual, unless he first wins it as a Jew, and "the prerequisite to the liberation of the individual is the liberation of the group to which he by birth belongs." Accordingly, "nationalistic Zionism demands not only group autonomy, but complete individual liberty for the Jew *as Jew*." Enlightenment has failed for the Jew because it offered him complete individual liberty on condition that he cease being a Jew; but "Zionism extends the principle of enlightenment by requiring for the Jew complete individual liberty not as an abstract human being of ambiguous nationality, but also as a Jew. Zionism asserts the principle of freedom of association."[39]

While in history Jews had been disfranchised and enslaved as a corporate entity, as a nationality, the Enlightenment and Napoleon offered them the franchise and liberty individually, "Jew by Jew, each as a 'natural man,' the equal of all other 'natural men,' without heredity, history, language, culture, or social memory. . . ." The offer stripped the Jews of all that made them concrete human beings, of all their reality. The Enlightenment and emancipation would remove all inferiorities, but also all differences. "The whole process," wrote Kallen in 1921, "rests on the illusion that equality is similarity."

As one can readily see, all the essential ingredients of what has come to be known as cultural pluralism were articulated by Horace Kallen in his attempt to define Hebraism and Zionism. On the published record, it would seem that he arrived at cultural pluralism by thinking about himself as a Jew and about the meaning and significance his Jewishness should have had for him. But as he thought about himself, he soon found himself thinking about the Jewish people, their literature, their history, their place in human history, and their future. In an essay on "Judaism, Hebraism, Zionism" published in 1910, Kallen wrote in general terms that "culture . . . constitutes a harmony, of which peoples and nations are the producing instrument, to which each contributes its unique tone, in which the whole human past is present as an enduring tension, as a background from which the present comes to light and draws its character, color, vitality."[40] Here is the analogy with the orchestra, and the harmony which was to become orchestration of the differences. But when the college student Kallen, under the influence of Barrett Wendell, turned to his Hebraic heritage, he had already been exposed to the strong influence of William James and the American tradition. "Every idea," Justice Oliver ·Wendell Holmes wrote, "is an incitement." A wise man possesses ideas; but ideas have a way of possessing a man, of pushing his mind in this or that direction. In Horace Kallen's case, the complex ideas that lodged in his mind fell into an order—intricate, dynamic, deep—in which ideas became strange bedfellows; in which the Hebrew Prophets, William James, Barrett Wendell, Louis D. Brandeis, Theodor Herzl, Moses Hess, Thomas Jefferson, James Madison, Thomas Paine, and Ralph Waldo Emerson, all were on friendly speaking terms and all seemed to have a part in Kallen's philosophy, which he called the American Idea, or cultural pluralism, or Hebraism. The name does not really matter, for the life of Kallenism, like the life of the man himself, was a self-evolving circle. In the beginning was its end, and in the end its beginning.

In Kallen's own order of priorities, Hebraism came first. Reflecting upon his own intellectual-moral development, Kallen wrote in 1933: "It is upon the foundation and against the background of my Jewish cultural milieu that my vision of America was grown."[41] It is not true, as has been asserted, that Kallen saw Zionism through his vision of America. The order, by his own published testimony, was just the reverse: he saw America through his vision of Zionism. He read the Declaration of Independence against his memory of the exile, as he and his people left Egypt for the Promised Land, slavery for freedom. "In our household," he wrote, "the suffering and slavery of Israel were commonplaces of conversation; from Passover to Passover, freedom was an ideal ceremonially reverenced, religiously aspired to. The textbook story of the Declaration of Independence came upon me, nurtured upon the deliverance from Egypt and the bondage in exile, like the clangor of trumpets, like a sudden light. What a resounding battle cry of freedom!"[42]

From his own experience Kallen evolved his views on education of Jews as Jews. The key to his philosophy of Jewish education was his understanding of the past, of tradition, and of its function in the life of the individual and his group. The basic idea, Goethe said, is that a tradition is not inherited as if it were a piece of property; it needs to be achieved as something for and on which one works. In the process of achieving a tradition, or a past, the person or the group changes that past, that tradition. A person or a group *makes* his or their past; and so the past is something that is constantly remade. And only insofar as the process of remaking takes place is the past or the tradition a living, not a dead, past or tradition. As Emerson put it in his essay on "Self-Reliance," a man lives *now*, and thus he "new dates" and "new creates" the whole. Thus the Bible, or Plato, or Homer has no significance, no life to a primitive man who lives in an African or Amazonian forest. They are part of my past, my tradition, only because they are part of my *present* life.

Kallen never tired of teaching this lesson in countless ways and forms. Explaining the meaning of tradition in *Cultural Pluralism and the American Idea* (1956), he wrote:

> That word means, literally, a carrying on, a continuous ongoing—but a carrying on, or ongoing, as any person's life goes on, not changelessly, but as a process of changing, where the old phases both continue in the new and are altered by the new. Self-preservation, whether of an individual or a group, is this process wherein the past endures only as it lives on in the present and future, and lives on only as it is changed by them.[43]

People say that they cannot change the past. But Kallen asked: "What else is there to change? What else is the present but the past changing?" Only what is dead does not change. "Unhappily, in our experience," wrote Kallen, "whatever stays truly always and everywhere the same stays null and dead. What exists and lives, struggles to go on doing so, and its struggle is its change. A living culture is a changing culture; and it is a changing culture . . . because of the transactions wherewith living, altering individuals transform old thoughts and things while laboring to preserve them and to produce new."[44]

Kallen saw in the application of this view to the Jewish tradition a self-transcending and self-transforming principle, without which that tradition would be dead. Without the built-in self-transforming principle, the Jewish people would, indeed, be what Arnold Toynbee falsely said they were, "a fossil of Syriac civilization." Through Jewish living and education Jewish culture has survived, "as the living past growing and changing in the present, making the newness of the future." For American Jews Kallen saw the possibility of growth and change in the interplay between Jew and non-Jew, each bringing to the union the rich cultural inheritance that the words "Jewish" and "American" suggest. As he put it in an essay written in 1955:

> Such consummations are beyond the reach of the individual isolate and alone. They require a home-centered community with its traditions of language, diet, worship, feasting and fasting, play and sport, expressive and representative arts, all carrying forward communal remembrance, beliefs, works and ways. . . . Their communication by the generations is what sustains the communion which holds the altering community together. They are what *Jewish* in *Jewish American* signifies. They thrive best when supported by a free trade with their peers of different communal cultures, assimilating and hence transfiguring what they get in exchange,

and again communicating the new life-form of their changing and growing old culture to their non-Jewish neighbors, and receiving theirs in return. The social orchestration which this intercultural exchange consummates actualizes the American Idea and gives the culture of the American people the qualities that Whitman and Emerson and William James and Louis Brandeis celebrated.[45]

Kallen said in this passage what he said over and over again, in his inimitable style, which was as personal as that of Henry James. What was that message? That the Jew is different by reason, not of his birth, but of his culture, which is the product of thousands of years of growth and development; that the Jew is not a Jew in isolation, but as a member of a communion and a fellowship that preserves, transmits, and changes Jewish tradition and culture; that the Jewish tradition and culture thrive best when they are not isolated but live in symbiotic relation with other cultures, with other traditions, in an orchestration based on the principles of the right to be different, of live and let live, live and help live. In this way, the individual Jew achieves inner peace and enjoys outer freedom, and a Jewish community constituted of such individual Jews enjoys happiness. The Jew, said Kallen,

. . . comes best to his personal health and wholeness amid a configuration of institutions which preserve, use, and transmit the knowledge, the ways and the works whereby a Jew is a Jew, and do so in the course of an open and free inter-communication of forms of faith, vision and works with the entire miscellany of communities and enterprises orchestrating into the American people and the American way. The orchestration liberates the Jewish person . . . for his optimal role in our national culture. By virture of it, his Jewishness is help and not hindrance, and his commitment to the Idea which renders America American is unrestricted and creative.[46]

Thus to be a creative American the Jew must be a Jew; and to be a Jew, he must be creative both as a Jew and as a human being, one who has inherent and inalienable rights, who has freedom and the right to be different, and therefore the right to be a Jew: to express his human essence as a Jew, to belong to the family of man as one who belongs to the family of Jews.

It was a grand and noble vision, seen by one who saw America as the Promised Land, but saw it with the eyes of one who had first seen the Promised Land of Israel. He was an American and a citizen of the world. But first and always he was a Jew—one who had left the slavery of Egypt and entered the freedom march to which there is no end.

Notes

1. The biographical facts are based on a long interview with Kallen by the author and the late Mrs. Dorothy Kuhn Oko, at Truro, Cape Cod, Massachusetts, in August 1964, which was later made a part of the oral history collection of the American

Jewish Committee; also on many conversations and on an extensive correspondence between Kallen and the author.

2. See Sidney Hook and M. R. Konvitz, eds., *Freedom and Experience: Essays Presented to Horace M. Kallen* (Ithaca, N.Y., 1947), p. viii.

3. The American Association for Jewish Education has become the Jewish Education Service of North America; the Jewish Teachers Seminary–Herzliah has become part of Touro College; the Farband Labor Zionist Order has, together with several other Zionist organizations, become the Labor Zionist Alliance.

4. Kallen, *Creativity, Imagination, Logic* (New York, 1973), p. vii.

5. Kallen, *William James and Henri Bergson* (Chicago, 1914), p. 11.

6. Ibid., p. 105.

7. Kallen, *Cultural Pluralism and the American Idea* (Philadelphia, 1956), p. 24.

8. Kallen, *James/Bergson*, pp. 173, 174, and 182.

9. H. M. Kallen and Sidney Hook, eds., *American Philosophy Today and Tomorrow* (New York, 1935), p. 271.

10. Kallen, *Culture and Democracy in the United States* (New York, 1924), p. 218.

11. Kallen, *Individualism, an American Way of Life* (New York, 1933), p. 142.

12. Kallen, *Cultural Pluralism*, p. 177.

13. Ibid., p. 181.

14. Ibid., pp. 86–87.

15. Kallen, *Individualism*, pp. 194–95.

16. For a full, detailed study of Kallen as a Zionist thinker and activist, especially in the years 1914–21, see Sarah Schmidt, "Horace M. Kallen and the Americanization of Zionism" (Ph.D. diss., University of Maryland, 1973).

17. Kallen, "The Promise of the Menorah Idea," *Menorah Journal* (Autumn–Winter 1962): 12.

18. The *Nation* articles were reprinted in Kallen, *Culture and Democracy*.

19. Kallen, "The Promise of the Menorah Idea," p. 11.

20. Ibid.

21. Kallen, *Culture and Democracy*, p. 11.

22. Cf. Ferdinand Tönnies, *Gemeinschaft und Gesellschaft* (1887), trans. as *Community and Association* (1955).

23. Kallen, *Culture and Democracy*, pp. 122–23.

24. Ibid., pp. 94, 123.

25. Ibid., p. 60. Cf. Sir Henry Maine, *Ancient Law* (1861).

26. Kallen, *Culture and Democracy*, p. 117.

27. Kallen, *Cultural Pluralism*, p. 181.

28. Kallen, *Individualism*, pp. 21, 22, 28, and 105.

29. Kallen, *Cultural Pluralism*, p. 25.

30. Kallen, *Culture and Democracy*, p. 63.

31. For a comprehensive treatment of Kallen's contributions to Jewish education, see Louis Kaplan, "Judaism and Jewish Education in Horace M. Kallen's Philosophy of Cultural Pluralism" (Ph.D. diss., Dropsie University, 1971.)

32. These ideas are developed in many of Kallen's writings, but see especially his book *The Education of Free Men* (New York, 1949), pp. 117 and 236 on the concept of orchestration; on equality of the different and the right to be different, pp. 23 and 110; on hyphenation, p. 182.

33. See ibid., chap. 10, "That You Can Change Human Nature."

34. Kallen, "Hebraism and Current Tendencies in Philosophy" (1909), reprinted in Kallen, *Judaism at Bay* (New York, 1932), pp. 7 and 15.

35. In *Judaism at Bay*, p. 10.

36. Ibid., p. 33.
37. Ibid., p. 77.
38. Ibid., p. 112.
39. Ibid., p. 116.
40. Ibid., p. 37.
41. Kallen, *Individualism*, p. 5.
42. Ibid., p. 7.
43. Kallen, *Cultural Pluralism*, p. 23.
44. Ibid., p. 55.
45. Kallen, "American Jews, What Now?" *Jewish Social Service Quarterly* 32 (Fall 1955): 27.
46. Ibid., p. 21.

Horace M. Kallen on War and Peace

LEWIS S. FEUER

As the First World War was drawing to a close, Horace M. Kallen, like his friends Thorstein Veblen, Walter Lippmann, and John Dewey, was writing peace plans. It was a time of exhilaration. Kallen felt that the "great masses of men," represented by the European Labor and Socialist parties were behind President Woodrow Wilson. He thought, indeed, that Wilson's "international vision" coincided with that of the Bolsheviks. Though the international capitalist classes, in his view, feared the Bolshevik Revolution as "a new thing and terrible thing," Kallen saluted the Russians for having helped "most of all" to make the war at last one "of democracy and by democracy."[1] Though he was troubled by the "religious character," as he called it, of the Bolshevik "theory of life," and thought their disregard of the "sinister character" of the German enemy would lead the Bolsheviks to catastrophe, he was cheered that they had won the preponderant influence upon "the plain people of Europe."[2]

Never had America's intellectuals felt so close to the powers that were shaping national policy as they did in 1918. Kallen became a member of a famed group called "The Inquiry," which had been born when President Wilson called on his adviser, Colonel Edward M. House, to organize a group of scholarly experts to help collect the facts and formulate the policies that would guide him during the making of the peace. With President Sidney E. Mezes of the City College as director, and Walter Lippmann as secretary, a distinguished group of scholars, including such men as George L. Beer, C. H. Haskins, W. L. Westermann, and Allyn A. Young, was enlisted, who became "a central committee" of authorities, exerting a powerful influence on the president.[3] Kallen was stirred by the opportunity to bring his philosophy to bear on the problem of achieving a durable world order.

To Kallen, it seemed that that precedent that should guide the world peace planners was that of the thirteen independent and sovereign American states who between 1776 and 1787 had welded themselves into a United States; "they were in precisely the same position and confronted precisely the same problems, in principle," he wrote, "as the present states and governments of the world."[4] The problems of international commerce, in his view, were those of "interstate commerce writ large." It was a question of writing "the ineluctable fact of the economic interdependence of mankind" into the law of nations.[5] International commissions, Kallen believed, could coordinate and distribute the world's food supply, keep open the world's highways, and secure the equality of all men before the law everywhere. And in the manner of the Articles of Confederation, the International Congress would decide the extent of each member state's armament, establish a commission for inspection and publicity, and bravely regard any violation of its rules as "tantamount to a declaration of war."[6] Filled with Wilsonian idealism, and with America's moral, economic, and military prestige world-high, Kallen and his fellow political philosophers felt that, led by Wilson, a political philosopher himself, they might inaugurate something like the rule of philosopher-kings. He placed much faith at this time in those whom he called "men of international mind,"[7] the elite of the world's intellectual class, such as Sidney Webb, H. N. Brailsford, G. Lowes Dickinson, John Dewey, Louis D. Brandeis, Thorstein Veblen, and notably the secretary of war himself, Newton D. Baker. When the New School for Social Research was founded in the spring of 1919, Kallen offered a seminar on "The International Mind: Its Nature and Conditions."[8] He hoped that these elite intellectuals, who for a quarter of a century had been advocating a league of nations, would dominate its founding conference as the fathers of the American constitution had dominated their convention in 1787. President Wilson had shown, in Kallen's eyes, by his "wise and firm course with regard to Mexico" how a great power could renounce any trace of an imperialist aim in its dealings with the weak.[9] The path to a rational world seemed clear. Indeed, to eradicate national prejudices, text books would be "internationalized"; an international commission would establish the objectivity, for instance, of the "facts" recorded in the handbooks of history.[10]

Perhaps now what impresses us most was the naïveté of the intellectual peace planners of 1918–19. Yet in politics all learning is by the trial and error method. To Kallen, the motto *E pluribus unum* engraved on American coins, and the principle of cultural pluralism seemed universal in its potential application. He minimized the cultural limits to cultural pluralism—the fact that the American colonies were composed of people almost all of whom spoke the same language, and believed in the same religion, and lived in a land blessed with plentiful uncultivated acres that beckoned to settlers. What would happen today in the United Nations if Kallen's one nation–one vote principle were instituted? Probably there would be an international act calling for the free migration of peoples on the earth's surface, and the terminating of all American restrictions on immigration. The right to choose one's domicile might be enacted into a human right, and traced to the wanderings of primitive tribes; the first tribal enclosure of land would, from the standpoint of the new ideology, have constituted the first private expropriation; millions of Asians and Africans would claim entry across America's borders. Kallen condemned the idea of sovereignty. "Sovereignty is international anarchy," he declared, "the ground of international rivalry, . . . of militarism."[11] Would its abrogation, however, not lead to a world-leveling of the advanced societies, a kind of "barracks communism," fatal to the excellences that he most prized?

We cannot have the same faith in international commissions that Horace Kallen had. Our experience with United Nations and UNESCO commissions has not been an altogether happy one; the recent attempt, for instance, to substitute government handouts for independent journalism was scarcely an inspiring one. What would a history of the world look like whose "facts" had to satisfy an International Commission with a Soviet and Third World majority? Increasingly, we are compelled to draw the distinction between *cosmopolitan* and *international*. The word *cosmopolitan* signifies, as the dictionary tells us, "belonging to all the world," "free from local, provincial, or national ideas, prejudices, or attachments . . .,"; whereas the word *international* signifies "pertaining to two or more nations"; it does not mean, as *cosmopolitan* does, a complete freedom from national prejudice; the Soviet and Third World blocs are international arrangements; they are not cosmopolitan.

It was possible for Kallen, like John Dewey, to be optimistic concerning the impact of the Soviet order on the peace of Europe. His journal of journeys, including one to the Soviet Union, was called *Frontiers of Hope* (1929).[12] Today its counterpart would more aptly be entitled *Frontiers of Hopelessness*. Hopeful in the future of the Jewish agricultural colonies in the Crimea, hopeful indeed that the *Yevsekzie*, the Jewish section of the Soviet Communist Party, would prove "the only effective guardians of the integrity of the Jewish inheritance in Russia, . . . the pioneers of a new way,"[13] Kallen praised "the wise nationalist policy of the Soviet Republic" that welcomed former Bundists and Zionists into the Jewish leadership. Yet he was disturbed that the latter practiced an anti-Semitism more "cruel" than that of their Gentile Bolshevik masters whom they wished to impress.[14] He was troubled when he heard that under Stalin, "a far from agreeable figure," anti-Semitism was on the rise again, and that the Jewish communists were concentrated in the opposition ranks. But he took heart when he encountered Maxim Litvinov, the Jewish Soviet foreign minister, at the Yiddish State Theater, looking exhausted, but enjoying a Yiddish play.[15] (What play could it have been?)

William James had taught his pupil Kallen that where the chance existed, "faith creates its own verification"; Kallen clung to the chance and the faith.

If that faith in the League of Nations and world peace was later nullified by events, it was not in Kallen's eyes falsified. He still thought with the advent of the Second World War that "the image of peace" drawn by the Treaty of Versailles was that of a freer society than had existed in 1914. The League of Nations had failed, he said, because the European governments, regarding it as the product of a "transatlantic illusionist," had reduced it into an instrument of power politics. Moreover, the intellectuals had shown a weakness of character; they had fashionably become cynics, debunkers, and Marxists. Kallen wrote a powerful passage: "Everywhere intellectuals, among them many of the experts who had been employed to construct the image of peace, began debunking both the faith of the war and the purposes of the peace. Cynicism as to motives, a sense of futility as to results, became the order of the day. Everywhere the forces of democracy suffered a failure of nerve, which expresed itself either in a flight into the communist illusion or in the form of pacifist declarations and vows never under any circumstances to fight in a war." The vogue of nonresistance, the "negativist pacifism" that enfeebled the West, made possible, in Kallen's judgment, "in no small measure," the assaults of Adolf Hiter on its civilization.[16]

With Kallen's indictment of the intellectuals, the overwhelming evidence compels agreement. One wishes that Kallen, himself an intellectual among intellectuals, had gone on to inquire into the attachment of intellectuals to the debunking and cynical ideologies with the same vigor that he brought to his inquiry into *Why Religion?*; he probably knew more diverse sections of the intellectual class than any man in his generation. But it is difficult to accept his view concerning the foundering of the League of Nations on the shoals of power politics. Perhaps it failed because it was not used for power politics. If America had joined the League, or entered into a security treaty with Britian and France, the first Nazi violations in the Rhineland zone could have been stopped. What kind of politics could have stopped Nazi aggression if not "power politics"? But influential liberal journals kept up a moralistic denunication of the League as an imperialist instrumentality. Even Herbert Croly denounced the Versailles Treaty as a Carthaginian peace, though clearly if it had been, the Nazi movement would never have arisen.[17] By 1924, *The New Republic* regarded the League as a "dead issue," and was supporting the radical isolationist, LaFollette, for the presidency;[18] Kallen had in 1918 sacrificed his post at the University of Wisconsin, perhaps needlessly, as Morris R. Cohen thought, in order to protest its limitation, during wartime, of LaFollette's freedom.

The chief alternative to such plans as Kallen's for the achievement of world peace was that advanced by Bertrand Russell. The English philosopher believed it would be best if the United States used its preeminent military and industrial power to organize the world as a whole, in other words, to act as the world's progressive imperalism, and do, for modern times, what Rome had done for its Empire, and what Alexander the Great had aspired to do for the Mediterranean and Asian states. "Intellectual anarchy," Russell argued, would not be resolved until "all the armed forces of the world are controlled by one world-wide authority," a measure that he believed could be brought about only probably "through the world government of the United States."[19] America's moral superiority seemd to him in 1922 unquestionable; "America," he wrote, "is definitely better, in international affairs, than any other Great Power. . . . America alone has stood for the independence and integrity of China. . . . America made a sincere effort to diminish the expense of naval armaments. . . . America showed, after the war, a complete absence of that hunger for territory which distinguished all other victors. These are very great moral assets, and they make me, in common with most European radicals, feel that, if any one power is to be supreme in the world, it is fortunate for the world that America should be that one."[20]

Two alternatives were thus posed, the confederational way to world government, or the unitary imperialist.[21] Perhaps if the United States had joined its economic and moral power in 1919 to that of its allies, a world government might have emerged. Or if it had availed itself in 1946 of its sole possession of the atomic bomb, it might through an ultimatum have compelled the democratization of the Soviet Union and the ouster of Stalin. In either case, it has become clear that the world peace can never be stable unless a government of constitutional liberties exists in every major country.

Even the Constitution of the United States sets a limit to the political pluralism allowable to the member states. According to Article IV, Section IV, the authors of the Constitution provided: "The United States shall guarantee to every state in this Union a Republican Form of Government, and shall protect each of them against Invasion. . . ." Theoretically, a political pluralist might have argued that if some given state, as Louisiana, for instance, had wished, in accordance with its Napoleonic, Spanish roots, to crown as its monarch King Huey I, it would have contravened political pluralism had the federal government ruled otherwise. Similarly, notwithstanding the Russian cultural sources for the Soviet dictatorship, the fact is that its suppression of individual rights (because it makes Soviet military and political planning into a completely secret process, hidden from the knowledge of a political opposition) poses a perpetual disequilibrating and anxiety-engendering force against world peace. Can the world's democratization be achieved without, indeed, the hegemony of an American imperialism? Kallen himself observed that the American constitution blundered in not going further in making war less likely among the states: "Force is the greatest need. . . . The insurance of lasting peace is force generalized into law."[22]

Indeed, the greatest force in the world making for peace may be less that of a cultural pluralism than what had best be called the "cultural Americanization" of the world. The world's culture is becoming American, and the world's language is becoming English; the simplicity of the English language is the most formidable weapon of American cultural imperialism. When I was in the Soviet Union, I met a group of Indonesian engineers training with some Soviet technologists; it transpired that they spoke to each other not in Russian but in English. English is becoming not only the *lingua franca* but the *lingua libertatis*. I have seen the phenomenon among Japanese peasants enjoying American Westerns and happy endings far more than their own traditional, ritually self-destructive dramas, and I have watched Melanesian, Javanese, and Tonkinese children on Pacific Islands drawn to the magic of the open-air films and baseball games in the American soldiers' camps. When Bertrand Russell, in 1924, reviewed Kallen's book, *Culture and Democracy in the United States*, he remarked that walking in Sicily, he had found every village "dominated by men who have returned from America, not only because they are richer, but because of the glamour and romance" attached to their reports of American "skyscrapers, subways, et cetera." And Russell added he had found "the same thing in Ireland, in the Tyrol, on the Volga, and wherever I have had the chance to test the feelings of peasants."[23] The Khomeinis of the world, trying to reinstate their pre-scientific cultures, are cultural diversities that scarcely "orchestrate" (in Kallen's favorite word) into a viable cultural pluralism.

To Kallen, of course, the notion of an American imperialism was altogether abhorrent. He disliked America's imperialist president, Theodore Roosevelt; he disliked him for his attacks on "hyphenated Americans," for his advocating the "melting pot," and for a vocation on behalf of the "national honor" that might provoke unnecessary wars.[24] In Kallen's eyes, Roosevelt was one of those "greedy and backward looking men" who shared a low conception of human nature;[25] what such "high priests" as Theodore Roosevelt called "human nature" was not "human nature" at all, said Kallen, but rather "second nature."[26] Kallen held to the liberal postulate, endorsed by John Dewey and Franz Boas, that with the growth of civilization, human nature would change; greed and war-lust, they foretold, would diminish greatly. Yet William James, Kallen's much venerated master, utterly disagreed with the liberal postulate. If God was no gentleman in James's sight, human nature was scarcely genteel.

Does one need to be reminded of William James's conception of man's nature? The " 'horrors' " of war, he wrote with his unflinching candor, "are a cheap price to pay for rescue from the only alternative supposed, of a world of clerks and teachers, of co-education and zoophily, of 'consumer leagues'. . . , of industrialism unlimited, and feminism unabashed." Without a stock of military characters at hand, the "mollycoddles," as Theodore Roosevelt called them, might make everything else disappear from the earth.[27] Our Darwinian heritage carved in zoological sculpture through long geological eras at the hands of the struggle for existence and natural selection could not be set aside by a liberal will-to-believe. As James put it: "History is a bath of blood. . . . Our ancestors have bred pugnacity into our bone and marrow, and thousands of years of peace won't breed it out of us. . . . [T]he martial virtues, although originally gained by the race through war, are absolute and permanent human goods." "The plain truth is that people *want* War. . . . War is human nature at its uttermost. . . . It is a sacrament. Society would rot without the mystical blood-payment."[28] For such reasons, James, like Freud after him, told the world's pacifists, that a warless world equilibrium would enervate men's spirits; even contemplating such a prospect for the indefinite future would induce "a deadly listlessness," the apprehension of a "stagnant summer afternoon" of a world without either "zest or interest."[29]

Nonetheless, William James, placing himself among the anti-imperialists and pacifists, proposed that they seek a "moral equivalent of war." In an inspiring sociological speculation that has been quoted only less often than his pragmatism, James envisaged the American youth conscripted for a few years in their lives in an army that was embattled with Nature; their Gettysburgs and Antietams would be fought not against fellowmen but amidst the dangers of mines and fishing fleets, handling the explosives in constructing tunnels and roads, and presumably in our own era, in navigating unvoyaged spaces, and landing upon bleak, friendless planets. "They would have paid their blood-tax, done their own part in the immemorial human warfare against nature. . . ."[30]

It was to James's teaching that Kallen returned as the Second World War deepened a hundred years after his birth: "To me the singularity of William James remains his call to arms in the immemorial war of freedom for every man, of which the present crisis is but the present phase."[31] Kallen, however, never seems seriously to have questioned whether a "moral equivalent of war" is possible, or to have inquired into the diverse kinds of consequences of its partial equivalents.

It took much experimentation to establish that there was indeed a determinate mechanical equivalent of heat. James, on the other hand, proceeded on a very slender empirical base when he proposed "the moral equivalent of war." For war channelizes the personal aggressive feelings directed against men, and it is not clear that such feelings can be converted into aggressive drives against nature. The "hard-hats" of the construction industry, who were risking their lives in dangerous physical labor, might, according to James's formula have been expected to be more pacifist than the students of the humanities; that was scarcely the case. Kallen himself disliked the aggression turned inward that disabled the pacifists, and thereby helped Hitler triumph to power. Lenin's conversion of an imperialist war to civil war educed a kind of "immoral equivalent" when one considers the bloodshed and extensive executions that followed for several decades.

Was it a sociological mutation, "the secret and the glory of our English speaking race," in James's words, that it possessed the habit of a "disciplined good temper" toward an opposite party that won fairly?[32] Are there some genetic mutations or Darwinian selections that have endowed some people with larger capacities for partial equivalents to war than others? To be sure, the Jews, devoted during many centuries to study, the peaceful arts and trade, became unmartial and defenseless. Yet even they finally accepted war as, under certain circumstances, a moral equivalent of wisdom and a reaffirmation of life. The transmutation of the ghetto bookworm into an Israeli soldier would have fascinated William James who wanted to write a *Varieties of Military Experience.*[33]

Psychological science has not advanced very much since James's time as far as its understanding of the limits of sublimation are concerned. Can aggressive energies be redirected from bellicose to constructive modes with the same degree of success or failure as sexual energies are sublimated into the arts and sciences? Or would the conquest of the environment provide something less than a one-to-one transformation for aggressive drives most naturally directed against human beings? And if such an equivalent transformation cannot be achieved, does the vocation of imperialist leadership offer the optimal means for sublimating aggressive energies in directions consistent with the advancement of civilization? The most relatively peaceful century, the nineteenth, was perhaps that in which aggressive energies were most successfully transmuted into great imperialist ventures. Such men as Rhodes, Barnato, Lugard, and Livingstone organized new industries, abolished slavery, and founded medical missions in jungles. On the other hand, this kind of transmutation of human energies would arouse little enthusiasm today. A Jamesian scheme today to enlist the youth would probably be vetoed; perhaps degenerate trends of the sort that Darwin's disciple, Sir Edwin Ray Lankester, investigated, now dissipate energies that otherwise might have been transformed constructively; degradation of energy ensues rather than its progressive enhancement.

For all his faith in the plasticity of human nature, Kallen's loyalty to Zionism was based in part on a skepticism concerning the extent to which the Enlightenment had really permeated the souls of Europeans. Kallen debated the issue of Zionism in a celebrated controversy with the City College philosopher, Morris R. Cohen, in the pages of *The New Republic*. Cohen charged that Zionism was incompatible with liberalism, that a Jewish state would become intolerant and illiberal as do all nationalist states, that Zionists believed the Jews were a superior race, and that though "Enlightenment is a painfully slow process,"[34] the assimilation of Jews that was its consequence for policy was the wisest counsel. To all this, Kallen responded that "what Mr. Cohen calls enlightenment has failed. . . ."[35] Was this not an avowal on Kallen's part that the forces of human unreason and destruction were far more deep-seated than the liberal philosophers and psychologists had believed? Although repudiating the doctrine of the "chosen people" in any version, Kallen argued that the individual would not be liberated until the group to which he belonged was liberated, and consequently, that only when Jews had their own homeland would they be equal with other peoples. Kallen's argument, moreover, seemed to acknowledge that democracies too can be intolerant of groups with divergent ways and beliefs, and especially so when the latter are defenseless; a homeland is an effective antidote to intolerance chiefly because it eradicates the image of the defenseless.

The tragic conclusion was, apart from all philosophical considerations, that if European Jewry had trusted less to either bourgeois liberalism or to working-class internationalism, that if, indeed, they had been more imbued with tribalism, the chances are that more of them would have survived the onset of the Nazi mass destruction. Also, it is difficult to see how the Hebraic culture that Kallen prized can resist the American circumpressures for assimilation unless it counterposes a conviction in a "chosenness," that is, a genetic-cultural superiority that would be relatively lost to mankind if it were dispersed in the general genepool. The survival of the Jews that Kallen sought seems to rest finally on an aversion to a Genetic Diaspora. If that is the case, one might ask how the democratic philosophy of equality might be accommodated to the existence of possible ethnic variations in mental or physical abilities, genetically grounded, through the sieves of the natural selective process itself.

Kallen's political outlook merged William James's voluntarism with Theodor Herzl's exhortation. His final words to the doubters and disbelievers in an International Society were: "Regard a free league of free peoples; if you will it, it is no dream."[36] The last words reiterated Herzl's stirring call to the first Zionist Congress. But was the state of Israel indeed achieved through a free act of will? The Zionist movement during the 1920s had declined to appallingly low numbers.[37] What revived it was the barbarian recrudescence of the Nazis. It took the combination of Hitler's assault upon European Jewry, together with the failure of the free world and the Soviet regime alike to take action to save the Jewish population, that engendered the remaining Jews' farewell to Europe, and their ingathering to Israel.[38] Would it, by analogy, require likewise the trauma of world catastrophe to induce the founding of a planetary league of free peoples? Otherwise, only an American Empire seems the remaining alternative that might approximate to a world federal republic.

Never daunted by metaphysical, or metahistorical problems, Kallen remained until the end of his life an optimist. He was still prepared, as he put it, to bet on the struggler rather than the event, though, on his own account, the odds would have been, and are, overwhelmingly against him. He rejected, however, any notion of immortality: "lives end with death; . . . their meaning perishes with them." He resolutely denied, nonetheless, that "extinction by dying rendered meaningless the living of life as it is lived,"[39] though Ecclesiastes would have disagreed, and, I think, rightly so. Empirical observation indicates that children, especially the affectionate ones, on first learning about death, are shocked by the news that all they love and their selves as well must die; frequently, in momentary despair, they internalize the inevitable, saying, "so let's all die together, and get it over with." I did once hear Kallen, as he was reflecting that he was "on the way out," refer gloomily to the efforts of philosophers as "a whistling in the dark." Logically, with the odds against him, Kallen should not have wagered on the human struggler unless he believed that some non-demon would intervene to affect (at least partially) the dice. But Kallen would not venture beyond recognizing the Joban impersonal flux of energies. How he founded his philosophy of freedom on this impersonal natural setting was never made clear. Presumably Job, choosing to maintain his integrity, acted of his free will; but how within the deterministic flux of energies had there arisen enclaves of freedom, partially exempt from physical laws? How explain these singularities of human freedom without a Jamesian hypothesis of a personal deity intervening to impinge its partial counterpart within the impersonal physical order? And if the latter physical flux is coextensive with reality, why should a Job, broken physically, and unable to reinstate his physical equilibrium, that is, his integrity, refuse to curse God, that totalistic physical flux, and die? But Kallen chose the mandate for life. Perhaps, in the ultimate pragmatic dealing with the unknown that lies at the heart of his philosophy, a belief in a personal God remained as an inarticulate premise; for the culture of the modern intellectual renders that premise inarticulate.

Indeed, an utter contradiction pervades Kallen's notion of an impersonal flux, for impersonal though it is, in his view, it makes for righteousness. And this latter attribute seems to endow the impersonal forces with a personal attribute. Kallen chose the Book of Job as the basic text for his Hebraism, yet Job, not a Hebrew himself, was scarcely representative of Hebrew thought. Kallen seems to have chosen Job because it was closest among biblical works to Russell's *A Free Man's Worship.* He acted the part of Job himself when his dramatic version of the book was performed in 1913 by the Wisconsin Players.[40] Could Hebraism provide enough of a distinctive religious basis to enable a culture to survive? Hardly so. Was the Hebraic spirit indeed more historically minded, as Kallen thought, than the Hellenic? Again not so if one recalls with Ecclesiastes that in the world of social affairs, "there is nothing new under the sun." Perhaps the international peace plans contravene Jewish social wisdom.

Notes

1. Horace M. Kallen, *The Structure of Lasting Peace: An Inquiry into the Motives of War and Peace* (Boston, 1918), pp. ix, x, 134.
2. Ibid., pp. 130–31.
3. Charles Seymour, ed., *The Intimate Papers of Colonel House* (Boston, 1928), 3:169, 170–72, 319. Also cf. Arthur D. Howden Smith, *Mr. House of Texas* (New York, 1940), p. 257. Sidney Ratner, ed., "Preface," in *Vision and Action: Essays in Honor of Horace M. Kallen on His 70th Birthday* (New Brunswick, 1953), pp. vii–viii.
4. Kallen, *The Structure of a Lasting Peace*, pp. 136–37.
5. Ibid., p. 54.
6. Ibid., pp. 166–67, 170.
7. Ibid., p. 162.
8. Horace M. Kallen, *What I Believe and Why—Maybe: Essays for the Modern World* (New York, 1971), p. 178. Actually the term had already been used by Nicholas Murray Butler in "The International Mind: How to Develop It," *Proceedings of the Academy of Political Science* 7(1971): 208–12. Cited in Albert K. Weinberg, *Manifest Destiny: A Study of Nationalist Expansionism in American History* (Baltimore, 1935), p. 540.
9. Kallen, *The Structure of a Lasting Peace*, p. 46.
10. Ibid., p. 176.
11. Kallen, *The Structure of a Lasting Peace*, p. 34.
12. Horace M. Kallen, *Frontiers of Hope* (New York, 1929).
13. Ibid., p. 394.
14. Ibid., pp. 393, 384, 386–87.
15. Ibid., pp. 320, 344.
16. Horace M. Kallen, *The Future of Peace*, Public Policy Pamphlet no. 34 (Chicago, 1941), pp. 35–36. But cf. Horace M. Kallen, *Zionism and World Politics: A Study in History and Social Psychology* (New York, 1921), p. 197.
17. Bruce Bliven, *Five Million Words Later: An Autobiography* (New York, 1970), p. 161. Also cf. Charles Forcey, *The Crossroads of Liberalism: Croly, Weyl, Lippmann, and the Progressive Era, 1900–1925* (New York, 1961), pp. 285, 302.
18. Bliven, *Five Million Words Later*, p. 243.
19. Bertrand Russell, in *Living Philosophies* (New York, 1941), pp. 18–19.
20. Bertrand Russell, "Hopes and Fears as Regards America," *The New Republic* 30 (15 March 1922): 70.
21. H. G. Wells similarly recognized two such basic alternatives in his "British Imperialism Foredoomed," *The New Republic* 60 (4 September 1929): 62–66. Like Kallen, he looked to "a new idea of world organization" superseding the divisive sovereignties. Othewise destructive wars would exhaust and degenerate our species.
22. Kallen, *The Structure of a Lasting Peace*, p. 152.
23. Bertrand Russell, "Americanization: Horace M. Kallen, Culture and Democracy in the United States," *The Dial* 77 (August 1924): 159, 160.
24. Kallen, *The Structure of a Lasting Peace*, pp. 182 ff.
25. Ibid., p. 183. Kallen even blamed the enactment of the Prohibition Amendment on the wish to exploit workingmen by making them more efficient, though he

strangely predicted that capitalism, through prohibition, was digging its own grave, because the workers, unable to dissolve their miseries in alcohol, would turn their resentments against capitalism. The decade of the twenties, however, was probably the most docile in the history of the labor movement.

26. Ibid., p. 185.

27. William James, *Memories and Studies* (New York, 1912), pp. 276–77.

28. Ibid., pp. 269, 272, 288, 304.

29. Ibid., p. 303. Also William James, *Talks to Teachers on Psychology; and to Students on Some of Life's Ideals* (New York, 1899), p. 270.

30. James, *Memories and Studies*, p. 291.

31. Horace M. Kallen, "Remembering William James," in *In Commemoration of William James: 1842–1942* (New York, 1942), p. 12.

32. James, *Memories and Studies*, pp. 60–61.

33. Ralph Barton Perry, *The Thought and Character of William James* (Boston, 1935), 2:272.

34. Morris R. Cohen, "Zionism: Tribalism or Liberalism?" *The New Republic* 18 (8 March 1919): 182–83. Reprinted in Morris R. Cohen, *The Faith of a Liberal: Selected Essays* (New York, 1946), p. 331.

35. Horace M. Kallen, "Zionism: Democracy or Prussianism?" *The New Republic* 18 (5 April 1919): 311–13. Reprinted in "Zionism and Liberalism," *Judaism at Bay* (New York, 1932), pp. 111–20.

36. Kallen, *The Structure of a Lasting Peace*, p. 187.

37. Before the First World War, wrote Leonard Stein, the Zionists "were looked upon by most of their fellow-Jews as unworldly dreamers out of touch with realities. . . . Great Britain, with a Jewish population of about 300,000 had in 1913 some 8,000 enrolled Zionists," while in 1913, "out of the three million Jews in the United States, only some 12,000 had enrolled themselves as Zionists." (Leonard Stein, *The Balfour Declaration* [New York, 1961], pp. 66–67.) In 1929, on the eve of the Depression, the membership of the Zionist Organization of America was little more than 18,000—a figure less than it had been in 1922. (Melvin I. Urofsky, *American Zionism from Herzl to the Holocaust* [New York, 1976], p. 287.) "Zionism was not a popular cause: it was never meaningful to the Jewish masses in the United States, only to a certain group of intellectuals." (Yonathan Shapiro, *Leadership of the American Zionist Organization, 1897–1930* [Urbana, 1971], p. 87.)

38. The many-tongued Andrei Gromyko summarized the facts in his speech as Soviet delegate to the United Nations General Assembly on 14 May 1947: "The Jewish people suffered extreme misery and deprivation during the last war. It can be said, without exaggeration, that the sufferings and miseries of the Jewish people are beyond description. . . . In the territories where the Hitlerites were in control, the Jews suffered almost complete extinction . . . something in the neighborhood of six million. . . . But these figures . . . give no idea of the situation in which the great mass of the Jewish people find themselves after the war . . . deprived of their countries, of their shelter, and of means of earning their livelihood. . . . The experience of the past, particularly during the time of the Second World War, has shown that not one state of Western Europe has been in a position to give proper help to the Jewish people. . . ." Andrei Gromyko, *A Palestine Solution* (New York, 1947), pp. 9–11.

39. Horace M. Kallen, *What I Believe and Why—Maybe*, p. 175.

40. Horace M. Kallen, *The Book of Job as a Greek Tragedy* (New York, 1918; new ed., 1959), p. xviii. Howard Mumford Jones, *An Autobiography* (Madison, 1979), p. 52.

Horace M. Kallen and Cultural Pluralism

SIDNEY RATNER

Every idea is an event in the biography of some individual, and if it is of any consequence, it is also an event in the life of that individual's cultural group and country. Horace M. Kallen's cultural pluralism was such an idea, which he first introduced in a class that he was teaching at Harvard around the year 1906 or 1907. He presented the idea to the general public in 1915 and developed the theme in various essays and books during the following sixty years of his life.[1]

Kallen first coined and publicly proposed *cultural pluralism* as a solution to an ideological conflict over Americanization. His proposal emerged from a momentous decision-making process that he, other immigrants, and old-line native Americans (white Anglo-Saxon Protestants) were engaged in then, and that we contemporary Americans still have to grapple with.

Cultural pluralism has been recognized as a major contribution to American philosophy. I should like to examine closely the social tensions that led to this proposal, to analyze the range of alternative solutions Kallen might have considered, and to assess some of the consequences of Kallen's decision.

Kallen was stimulated to evolve his theory of cultural pluralism by the white Anglo-Saxon Protestant reaction against the massive wave of immigration from southern and eastern Europe between 1890 and 1914. In the fifteen years preceding America's entrance into World War I, the United States had received nearly 13 million immigrants of whom nearly 75 percent were from southern and eastern Europe. Many of them were poor manual workers, forced to live in the slums of American cities. This influx of immigrants of non-"Nordic" stock and the outbreak of World War I led to two movements: to Americanize the "new" immigrants and to restrict drastically on a quota basis the immigrants from eastern and southern Europe.

The concept of Americanization was formulated as early as the eighteenth century when Crèvecoeur wrote of Americans as new men, not duplicates of any European people, but a new stock created by a merger of many different strains. "Here, individuals of all nations are melted into a new race of men, whose labors and posterity will one day cause great changes in the world."[2]

During the nineteenth century, the open-door policy on immigration had been sustained by the belief of the majority of Americans that all the new immigrants could be absorbed and that each group would contribute to the emerging national character. This process of immigrant adjustment through assimilation of the ethnic groups already established on the American scene was given the striking image of the melting pot. Ralph Waldo Emerson during the 1850s opposed the anti-immigrant, anti-Catholic Know-Nothing party and acclaimed what he called a "smelting pot." "Man is the most composite of all creatures. . . . in this continent—asylum of all nations—the energy of Irish, Germans, Swedes, Poles, and Cossacks, and all the European tribes—of the Africans, and of the Polynesians will construct a new race, a new religion, a new state, a new literature, which will be as vigorous as the new Europe which came out of the smelting pot of the Dark Ages, or that which earlier emerged from . . . barbarism. *La Nature aime les croisements.*"[3]

Between the 1850s and 1908, few American writers explicitly used the analogy between the United States and a "melting pot." Most statements on the American people's prowess in the assimilation of new immigrant groups imply that the process occurred spontaneously and effortlessly. But in 1908, Israel Zangwill, an English novelist and playwright who knew the United States well, wrote a play, *The Melting Pot*, which made the term and the idea part of American language and thought. In this play the hero announces that "America is God's Crucible, the great Melting Pot where all the races of Europe are melting and reforming! . . . the real American has not yet arrived, he is only in the Crucible, I tell you—it will be the fusion of all races, the coming superman."[4]

The ideal of assimilation affirmed by Zangwill was also held and argued for forcibly in widely read books by such writers as Jacob Riis, Edward Steiner, and Mary Antin, as well as by such an eminent statesman as Theodore Roosevelt. On the other hand, even before the end of the nineteenth century, various publicists and scholars were arguing that Americans were fundamentally Anglo-Saxons, descendents of the British people; they contended that the new immigrants from non-English parts of Europe should adapt themselves to the already established institutions and ways of life in America. The white Anglo-Saxon Protestant model of behavior and character was to be the framework within which all the "new" immigrants were to be assimilated within the economy, political system, and culture. Some racist writers, such as Professor E. A. Ross and Madison Grant, in the early 1900s, asserted that the purity of the old Anglo-American stock was being destroyed by the immigrants from eastern and southern Europe. This view foreshadowed the restrictive legislation on immigration in the 1920s that was to discriminate so strongly against the "new" immigrants in favor of the "old" immigrant stocks in the United States.[5]

Against the strong pressures exerted on the "new" immigrants by the advocates of Americanization, the grey conformism of the melting-pot image, and the glorification of the Anglo-American stock, one person took the lead in offering a new vision of the rightful place and dignity of the allegedly inferior immigrant groups from eastern and southern Europe. That person was Horace M. Kallen. In 1915, at the age of thirty-two, a brilliant but academically insecure teacher of philosophy at the University of Wisconsin, he took the initiative in challenging the view that all the cultural groups who came to the United States were destined in the long run to become merged into one homogeneous mass and that it was desirable for all immigrants to divest themselves of every vestige of their own native culture. In a series of important articles published in 1915 and later elaborated in 1924 in his influential volume, *Culture and Democracy in the United States*, he developed an alternative program of action for all the immigrant groups under attack, based on the philosophy now famous as *cultural pluralism*. As he saw it, Americanization in the most liberal sense of the term involved not the destruction of all the distinctive cultural group traits other than those of the dominant Anglo-Saxons, but the cherishing and preserving of every ethnic group's cultural heritage—language, art, literature, music, customs—within the overarching framework of a common use of the English language and adherance to the prevailing political and economic system. Primary to this principle was a respect for democracy and a high concern for the importance of each individual. Kallen believed that individuality was enhanced when each individual functioned both as a member of his ethnic-cultural group and as a member of the larger American society that embraced all the divergent ethnic cultural groups within the United States. Instead of the widely used metaphor of the melting-pot, he offered the strikingly apt and fresh metaphor of the orchestra, with each instrument likened to a cultural group making its unique contribution to the symphony of civilization.

Perhaps the most compact statement of his program for a democratic culture and commonwealth in the United States would be the following:

> Its form would be that of a federal republic; its substance a democracy of nationalities, cooperating voluntarily and autonomously through common institutions in the enterprise of self-realization. . . . The common language of the commonwealth . . . would be English, but each nationality would have for its emotional and involuntary life its own peculiar dialect or speech, its own individual and inevitable esthetic and intellectual forms. The political and economic life of the commonwealth is the single unit and serves as the foundation and background for the realization of the dis-

tinctive individuality of each *nation* that composes it and of the pooling of these in a harmony above them all. Thus "American Civilization" may come to mean the perfection of the cooperative harmonies of "European Civilization" . . . an orchestration of mankind.[6]

Horace Kallen's cultural pluralism received a warm response from leading intellectuals like John Dewey, Randolph Bourne, and Norman Hapgood. In an important letter to Kallen (31 March 1915) John Dewey wrote about the harmonizing[7] implications of Kallen's metaphor of orchestration:

> . . . I want to see this country American and that means the English tradition reduced to a strain along with others. It is convenient for "the Americans" to put the blame of things they don't like on the "foreigners," but I don't believe that goes very deep; it is mostly irritation that some things they don't like and an unwillingness to go below the surface. I quite agree with your orchestra idea, but on condition we really get a symphony and not a lot of different instruments playing simultaneously. I never did care for the melting-pot metaphor, but genuine assimilation *to one another*—not to Anglo-Saxonism—seems to be essential to an America. That each cultural section should maintain its distinctive literary and artistic tradition seems to me most desirable, but in order that it might have the more to contribute to others. I am not sure you mean more than this, but there seems to be an implication of segregation geographical or otherwise. We should recognize the segregation that undoubtedly exists is requisite, but in order that it may not be fastened upon us.[8]

From 1915 to the present certain writers on cultural pluralism have criticized Kallen for alleged shortcomings in his theory. Most of these criticisms are ill-founded, based on either misreadings or careless readings of Kallen's writings, either those of 1915, or those written later. Let me state some of the qualifications to the theory of cultural pluralism that Kallen was conscious of and took account of in the corpus of his varied works. First, he explicitly stated that adherence to democracy, to liberty and union, by every ethnic-cultural group in America was necessary if cultural pluralism was to prevail. As he put it shortly after World War II, authentic democrats recognize the "equal right of different individuals and different associations of individuals to 'life, liberty and the pursuit of happiness.' Their device is E pluribus unum."[9] Second, Kallen realized how important the dependence of each individual upon his own group's culture was as a basis for that individual achieving his full potential as a distinctive personality. Ruth Benedict and other anthropologists have made this fact a commonplace in the last few decades, but it was not so widely appreciated before the 1930s. Third, Kallen was also conscious of the possible tyranny of a cultural group over any single individual and the desirability of each individual to interact with other cultural groups in order to be a fully rounded personality within the larger society of which he and his own ethnic group were parts. In 1952, Rabbi

Mordecai M. Kaplan wrote to Kallen: "I have always regarded you as the foremost creative American Jewish thinker who demonstrates by actual example that it is possible to live with distinction in two civilizations."[10]

Fourth, Kallen in the period between 1915 and 1924 argued forcibly that each member of an ethnic group is bound to that ethnic group by his biological heritage and the social relations he had with his relatives and kin from childhood through maturity. As he phrased it, in all these relations each member of an ethnic group "lives and moves and has his being." Fifth, Kallen built upon this empirical observation the normative criterion of the desirability of such ethnic identification by each individual. This value judgment was widely shared in the 1910s, and is still shared by many Americans today. But it should be recognized that there have always been individuals and certain sub-groups, especially cosmopolitan intellectuals like Walter Lippmann, who have consciously dissociated themselves from the ethnic group from which they came, and sought to be accepted by the Anglo-American group with whom they hoped to identify themselves.[11]

Sixth, Kallen was a pioneer in presenting his judgment and prediction about the indestructibility of ethnic cultures in the United States. This position contradicted the views of such authorities on assimilation as Isaac Berkson in *Theories of Americanization* (1920), Julius Drachler in *Democracy and Assimilation* (1920), and Robert E. Park and Herbert A. Miller in *Old World Traits Transplanted* (1921).[12] Kallen also made a value judgment and a social commitment when he urged his readers to take a stand for the permanent preservation of all ethnic group attachments, languages, and loyalties that were not in conflict with loyalty to the United States.[13]

One limitation in Kallen's theory of cultural pluralism that most writers fail to be aware of, is his almost excessive concentration on the cultural life of ethnic minorities and his failure to analyze in depth the generally inferior position of ethnic minorities in the then prevailing economic and political system. He was keenly aware of these problems of power and status, but had great faith in the ability of these groups to improve their economic welfare and political position as they achieved prosperity, education and pride in their own ethnic cultural heritage.[14]

Another limitation in Kallen's early writings on cultural pluralism was his failure to deal with the problem of integrating black Americans into American society. One of Kallen's critics asked: "Could anyone have designed a pluralism that would have suited Blacks as well as Jews [and Germans, Irish, Poles, Russians, and Scandinavians], the minorities that were left behind as well as those that were thriving? Could anyone, for that matter, have built a pluralist philosophy on the black experience?"[15] Professor John Higham's negative answer to this question was based in large part on his study of W. E. B. Du Bois, the leading ideological spokesman for many American blacks in the first few decades of the twentieth century. But Higham ignored the work of Alain Locke, the leading American black philosopher from the 1930s to the time of his death in 1954. Locke had been a student of William James, George Santayana, and Horace Kallen at Harvard in the early 1900s. Locke felt keenly the isolation and separation of black Americans from the rest of American society. But between 1935 and 1947, he too came to accept and to develop cultural pluralism as a philosophy for black Americans. Kallen's writings, teaching, and friendship undoubtedly influenced Locke, but the latter was a strongly independent person and developed this philosophy on his own in response to the needs of his fellow blacks. One of Locke's achievements was his pointing out that the Negro problem was a creation of non-Negroes, which they imposed on the Negroes. Kallen himself in his 1956 volume, *Cultural Pluralism and the American Idea* extended his cultural pluralism to include both the blacks and the American Indians.[16]

There is no doubt that *Culture and Democracy in the United States* is Horace Kallen's major contribution to the philosophy of cultural pluralism, and hence has received the greatest attention. Yet Kallen, despite his many important writings on other subjects, ranging from art and the consumers movement to peace, war, and Zionism, continued to develop new aspects of this theory. One notable work in this direction is Kallen's *Cultural Pluralism and the American Idea;*[17] another is his essay, "The American Dream and the American Idea," which appeared in *What I Believe and Why—Maybe;* and a third is a speech he gave in February 1963 on his philosophy of cultural pluralism, which was published in *Farband* (Labor Zionist Order) *News* (February 1963).

Each of these works embodies some significant new ideas that modify Kallen's earlier theses in one important way or another. I can only highlight a few of these innovations. The first involves Kallen's expansion of his earlier thesis that the validity and effectiveness of cultural pluralism, both as an idea and as a social institution, depend on each ethnic cultural group's valuing and participating in the policies and practices of American democracy. In his 1956 book, Kallen stresses this interdependence and goes on to explicate in detail his ideal of democracy, which he calls "the American Idea" and which he believes is the dominant theme of American history from Thomas Paine, Jefferson, and Washington through Emerson, Thoreau, and Whitman, to Josiah Royce, William James, and John Dewey.

The heart of the American Idea, as Kallen saw it, was embodied in four revolutionary theses set forth in the Declaration of Independence. The first was that all men are created equal; the second, that "life, liberty, and the pursuit of happiness" are every man's unalienable rights; the third, that government is a means and not an end, that its duties are to "secure these rights" and that it governs by the consent of the governed; and the fourth, that when government neglects or fails to perform the services for which it was devised, the people who instituted the government may "alter or abolish it" and replace it with a "new government."

To cynics, these statements are a collection of "glittering generalities," or "a salad of illusions." Kallen was acutely and painfully conscious that there have been throughout American history many powerful groups that have been vehemently opposed to these doctrines of equality and have defended the enslavement of the Negroes, the exploitation and partial extermination of the American Indians, and the treatment of Irish and non-Western European immigrants as inferior to the dominant Anglo-American settlers. Nevertheless, he thought that the slow, painful, and checkered movement for racial equality for the blacks from the Abolitionist movement, the Civil War, and the Reconstruction period to the Civil Rights victories in the Supreme Court and Congress from the 1940s to the 1970s, indicated that over the long haul the champions of democracy were realizing some of the ideals of the Declaration of Independence. He also took pride in the success of the women's rights movements, the slow, often violent struggles of labor unions to improve the conditions of workers in American industry, and the advances of different ethnic minority groups in achieving some recognition by the dominant Anglo-American groups. Finally, Kallen rejoiced in the fact that the International Declaration of Human Rights, which the Assembly of the United Nations adopted in 1948, was based on key ideas from the Declaration of Independence and was in harmony with his philosophy of cultural pluralism.[18]

The second important innovation that Kallen made after World War II was best put in his 1963 speech to the *Farband*—the Labor Zionist Order. In this speech, Kallen reaffirmed that each one of us, "so long as we live and that means so long as we keep on struggling to stay alive, is an indefeasible individual." Then he went on to qualify, if not to deny, the stress on biological heredity as a basis for group identification that he had made in his 1915 article and his 1924 book, *Culture and Democracy in the United States.* Kallen now asserted: "There are no born Jews any more than there are born Americans or born Englishmen. A newly born baby is a potential animal organism. What kind of human being it becomes is a matter of its basic experiences when it is at the mercy of the adults on whom it depends for its survival. In a Jewish household a neutral baby, whether the biological heritage is Chinese or Irish or even that of the descendents of the Daughters of the American Revolution, will grow up Jewish. A child of Jewish parents brought up in the context of the culture of a Chinese or a Russian or another community will grow up into that kind of person."

Kallen went on to stress the importance of culture and education. "The culture works as an educative process. In the early days the education is indirect. It comes by contagion, from the feel of the person, from the tone of voice in which it is addressed. It comes from the unconscious experiences, unverbalized, that the child is not aware of. Then the school supplements it; languages come in."

He concluded that every member of a cultural group, in order to be an effective member of that group had to know the history and varied aspects of that culture. Hence so far as any culture is concerned, especially the culture of people like the Jews, "education is survival, survival is education." To Kallen, the acquisition of one's cultural heritage involved that each member of a cultural group relate his personal memory and group memory to the development of his own personality. That person should relate his perception of his life experiences to group tradition. On certain occasions, he should welcome innovation to enhance the welfare both of his group and of himself.[19]

The third major innovation that Kallen made in his cultural pluralism involves the question of the explicit recognition of race by the courts in the 1960s and 1970s. In his 1971 semiautobiographical volume, *What I Believe and Why—Maybe*, Kallen recognized the humanitarian intent of Justice John M. Harlan when he stated in an opinion in 1896, that the U.S. Constitution is "color-blind." Kallen pointed out that "color-blind" became a slogan in the 1960s. President Lyndon Johnson in his speech in the early 1960s said, "until education is unaware of race, until employment is blind to color, emancipation may be a proclamation but it is not a fact." But Kallen pointed out that the metaphor "color-blind" brings an ominous self-deception. Actually, the Declaration of Independence and the Constitution with the Civil War Amendments assert the ungrudging acceptance of "color" in all its relations; "they postulate equality in rights and freedoms for the differents *as* differents." Here Kallen showed a keenness of insight and a courage in going against the main currents of his age that younger men might well have envied. A noted authority on the Supreme Court expressed his agreement with Kallen on this point; he asserted that the Negro or the white man will enjoy equal liberty in fact as well as in law only when he may, *as* Negro or *as* white man, *as* Jew or Catholic or Mormon "exercise and perfect his own powers at his own risk, without privilege and without penalty."[20]

Admirable as any philosophical theory may be in merit, the question always arises: how influential or effective was it? The answer involves viewing Kallen's theory in the context of the changes in American society from World War I to the present.

After Kallen's 1915 *Nation* articles appeared, two noted journalists and one famous philosopher were sufficiently influenced by Kallen's ideas to publish important articles in line with his cultural pluralism approach. Randolph Bourne, a brilliant critic of American culture and society, argued in an article entitled "Trans-National America," that Americanization was becoming ineffective because the Anglo-American ruling group excluded immigrants from full participation in various walks of life. He proposed a federation within the United States of the various immigrant groups as "threads of living and potential cultures." He saw a "trans-national" America becoming the world's first really international society. His tragic death a few years later at the age of thirty-two prevented his vision from being embodied in a more complete form and from reinforcing Kallen's ideas.[21]

Another influential publicist, Norman Hapgood, supported Kallen's line of thought in 1916, by urging Jews not to give up their distinctive cultural legacy. He went so far as to voice the hope that in the United States Americans might have "twenty different kinds of civilization, all harmonious."[22]

That same year, 1916, John Dewey made a powerful plea for a national unity "created by drawing out and composing into a harmonious whole the best, the most characteristic, which each contributing race and people has to offer." He argued that such terms as Irish-American, or Hebrew-American, or German-American are false terms because they seem to assume something that is already in existence called America, to which the other factor may be externally hitched on. The fact is, he asserted, the genuine American, the typical American, is "international and interracial in his make-up. . . . The point is to see to it that the hyphen connects instead of separates."[23]

During World War I, a liberal international approach to American nationalism was regarded by Wilsonian liberals as the domestic equivalent or complement of a federated world. National governmental agencies in Washington, D.C., especially the Committee of Public Information, applied this liberal approach. The Committee encouraged immigrant nationalities in the United States to relate the "best interests" of their native lands with the American cause.[24]

Unfortunately, the advances hoped for by Kallen and other champions of a pluralistic society were more than counterbalanced by the activities of the proponents of the Americanization movement. Their pressures against immigrant cultural identity reached a peak during the release of intense nationalistic feelings in World War I and the postwar "Red scare." The revival of the Ku Klux Klan in 1915 was one nativist manifestation of this emotionalism. Another was the restrictive immigration legislation of 1921 and 1924, based on "national origins" criteria unfavorable to the southern and eastern European immigrants. The rejection by the Anglo-Americans of their "new" immigrants resulted in these groups' expressing their outrage and anger. They waged a long campaign to abolish the national origins system and finally met with success with the Immigration and Naturalization Act of 1965, during Lyndon Johnson's presidency.

But, paradoxically enough, after the passage of the 1924 Immigration Act, wide public interest in assimilation and ethnic diversity began to decrease. Many of those who wrote sympathetically about cultural pluralism transformed it into a liberal rapprochement with Americanization, one that encouraged immigrants to preserve their cultural diversity during a period of additional adjustment. Yet this same liberal position was also favorable to eventual assimilation and the increase in national cultural unity.

During the 1920s many intellectuals became increasingly concerned about the power of the Ku Klux Klan, the rise of a virulent anti-Semitism promoted by Henry Ford and other powerful individuals, the strong anti-Catholic feeling among many Protestants shown in the 1928 presidential election, and an increased evidence of the disabilities experienced by Negroes. This concern was enhanced by the rising tide of racialism in Europe, especially in Germany.

Outstanding leaders in the fight against racialism in America were Franz Boas and Ruth Benedict in anthropology, and Robert Park and Louis Wirth in sociology. In general, these writers were sympathetic to Kallen's stress on the value of cultural diversity, but several tended to differ from him in stressing the desirability of ethnic merging or assimilation. This goal of cultural assimilation was stressed by the Swedish economist, Gunnar Myrdal, in his very influential book on race relations, *An American Dilemma* (1944). As he saw it, cultural assimilation was the normal experience of American ethnic groups, one that the nation's basic ideals set as a goal for all minorities regardless of race. Taking this stand, he rejected the claim made to him by Franz Boas's disciple, Melville Herskovits, that American Negroes had preserved over the centuries a distinctive African heritage, which they ought to cherish. Myrdal instead accepted the argument by Robert Parks's student, E. Franklin Frazier, that the Negro should be studied as an American type and as an American issue. Basically, Myrdal reasserted the validity of developing a program of cultural assimilation for all minority groups in the United States.[25]

World War II created an urgent need for improving intergroup relations in the United States. Kallen's cultural pluralism gained increased currency both as a term describing the actual existence of diverse cultural groups, and the belief that such ethno-cultural variety was good, as long as it did not involve ethnocentrism, prejudice, or discrimination among the various groups. Some advocates of cultural pluralism, however, did not realize that although cultural pluralism was an alternative to assimilation, it also involved an adherence to and strengthening of national unity, a consensus widespread enough to prevent serious tensions among the different ethno-cultural groups. A notable attempt to bridge the differences between pluralism and assimilation was made by Robert M. MacIver, a distinguished British-American sociologist. In the 1940s, he presented in several books, especially in his major work, *The Web of Government*,[26] a view of democracy as a unifying framework that permits a maximum of cultural diversity. By limiting the role of the state, democracy promotes, instead of hindering, the desirable differences among cultural groups without endangering national unity. This position of MacIver's was in fundamental harmony with Kallen's ideas.

From the mid-1940s through the 1950s and 1960s various social scientists made new approaches to both the melting-pot image and the theory of cultural pluralism. In 1944 and 1952, the sociologist Ruby Jo Reeves Kennedy presented a drastic revision of the melting-pot process in America, based on studies of intermarriage trends in New Haven from 1870 to 1940. She found that there was a distinct tendency for the British-Americans, Germans, and Scandinavians to marry among themselves—within a Protestant "pool"; for the Irish, Italians, and Poles, to marry among themselves, a Catholic "pool"; and for the Jews of one group—Sephardic, German, or Russian—to marry Jews from the other national groups. Although intermarriage was taking place across lines of different nationality backgrounds, the dominant tendency was for it to be confined within one or the other of the three major religious groups—Protestants, Catholics, and Jews. Hence, the situation in New Haven was better characterized as a "triple melting pot" based on religious differences, than as a "single melting pot." Mrs. Kennedy concluded that "while strict endogamy is loosening, religious endogamy is persisting and the future cleavages will be along religious lines rather than along nationality lines as in the past. If this is the case, then the traditional 'single-melting-pot' idea must be abandoned and a new conception which we term the 'triple-melting-pot' theory of American assimilation, will take its place as a true expression of what is happening to the various nationality groups in the United States."[27]

This triple melting-pot theory was adopted by the theologian Will Herberg, and was the basic sociological reference frame for his analysis of religious trends in American society, expressed in his well-known book *Protestant-Catholic-Jew.*[28] As he pointed out, it is *expected* in American society that all Americans are either Protestant, Catholic, or Jew, whether they are formally connected with the church or synagogue, or not. Although the American ethnic group, as he saw it, may eventually lose its distinct identity, its functions are taken over by a religious community. Religion is then seen as the enduring dimension of diverse ethnic cultures and the basis of American pluralism. This view had considerable popularity in the 1950s when a religious revival was under way, but as this revival declined in the 1960s, social scientists turned to a new basis for ethnic pluralism patterns of social behavior.

Milton Gordon, in a path-breaking book, *Assimilation in American Life,*[29] retained the key ideas of Kallen's cultural pluralism but distinguished sharply between cultural elements and social group activity patterns. He pointed out that many members of ethnic cultural groups were losing their languages and customs, yet persisted in having more frequent and intimate social relations with one another than they did with persons who did not belong to their ethno-cultural group. In a later work in the 1970s, he stressed the importance of social-class divisions that cut across ethnic group lines and minorities just as they do those of the white Protestant population in America. These class divisions in minority groups tended to restrict interpersonal relations within these groups because the members of each class felt more comfortable in intimate social relations with those who shared their own class background or attainments. Gordon's final conclusion was that cultural assimilation had taken place in America to a greater extent than Kallen had anticipated or desired but that diverse ethnic groups persisted as distinct social groups in part because of religion or race, in part because of cultural differences.[30]

In contrast to the works in the 1940s and 1950s that asserted that a decrease in the strength of cultural pluralism was occurring in the United States, a number of influential books appeared in the 1960s and 1970s, that treated the survival and renewal of cultural pluralism under a new name, *ethnicity*. Their themes won the widespread approval of different minority groups as the black civil rights movement and the Vietnam War increased tensions and created new cleavages in American society. One pioneer scholarly book in this new trend was Nathan Glazer and Daniel Moynihan's *Beyond the Melting Pot: The Negroes, Puerto Ricans, Jews, Italians, and Irish of New York City.*[31] Their thesis was that ethnicity is a permanent quality of American society, particularly in cities. In their eyes, the hopes of the champions of the melting-pot process a half-century ago for an ultimate fusion of the American people have not been realized. Although immigration on a large scale from Europe ceased in the 1920s, and today's Jews, Italians, and Irish are quite different from their European parents and grandparents, these ethnic groups have persisted. Actually, events during the past three decades stimulated the tendency to adhere in ethnic clusters. According to Glazer and Moynihan, ethnic groups in the United States are continually recreated by new experiences in America, especially through ties of family, friendship, and economic interest. Common concerns about employment, economic opportunity, housing, and other important social questions lead members of an ethnic group to act together as pressure groups and live together as social groups.

Perhaps the most controversial book on the "new ethnicity" was Michael Novak's *The Rise of the Unmeltable Ethnics: Politics and Culture in the Seventies.*[32] The author agreed with Glazer and Moynihan that America was not a melting pot and that it was time for a new cultural pluralism and politics based on this cultural pluralism. But Novak came under sharp attack for attempting to justify the hostilities between groups of white Americans and blacks, while at the same time proclaiming that lower class ethnics and blacks are allies. He stressed what he took to be the undying opposition between the WASPs and the sensibilities of such ethnic groups as Slovaks and Italians.

In opposition to such strident championship of the white ethnic groups in the United States was Alphonso Pinkney's *Red, Black and Green: Black Na-*

tionalism in the United States.[33] This volume was a scholarly review of the developments of black nationalism in the United States with special attention to the role of Malcolm X, the Black Panther party, the cultural nationalism of blacks like Baraka, and the religious nationalism of blacks that expressed itself in "the Nation of Islam." The book was also an affirmation of the Chinese communist position that "in the final analysis, national struggle is a matter of class struggle."

During the late 1970s and early 1980s, several scholars, for example, Gunnar Myrdal, voiced their opposition to the rhetoric and program of the advocates of what they called *romantic ethnicity.* Two powerful presentations of this new critical approach were made by Howard F. Stein and Robert F. Hill in *The Ethnic Imperatives*[34] and by Stanley Steinberg in *The Ethnic Right.*[35] Nevertheless, extensive support for ethnic cultural diversity among blacks and different white ethnic groups still persists and seems likely to endure into the foreseeable future.

The question then arises: To what extent has Horace Kallen's formulation of cultural pluralism been validated or impugned by developments in American society over the past seven decades? We must recognize that the restrictive immigration legislation of the 1920s resulted in a marked decrease in the number of ethnic minority group members who know their parents' or grandparents' native language, arts, and customs. Kallen had feared such legislation, but had hoped it would not be enacted. On the other hand, the Holocaust, the creation of Israel as an independent state, and the Arab-Israeli wars from 1948 to 1981 created a new sense of ethnic identity for most American Jews. Similarly, Soviet Russia's military domination of Eastern Europe created, among Poles, Hungarians, Yugoslavs, and other East European groups in America, a new concern and consciousness of their ethnic-cultural heritage. Still other ethnic groups (e.g., Italians, blacks, Mexican-Americans, Puerto Ricans, American Indians) responded to internal social conditions involving employment, housing, education, and civil rights by militantly asserting ethnic minority claims against the dominant ethnic groups in America. However controversial their protests and programs were and are, there is no doubt that the preservation of some form of cultural pluralism by these groups seems assured.

Such developments confirm Horace Kallen's belief that ethnic minority groups would cherish their distinctive cultural traits and feel it desirable to do so, in one way or another. These groups have also operated within the overarching framework of a common use of the English language and adherence to the prevailing political and economic systems. Kallen postulated a respect for democracy and a high concern for the importance of each individual. Unfortunately, the passions aroused in the 1960s by the Vietnam War and the black civil rights movement led some extreme black and white groups to actions that violated the established democratic procedures and pitted group rights against individual rights in an extreme form. Kallen was sympathetic to some of the goals of most of these groups, but deplored and would have continued to deplore the use of antidemocratic strategies and the rigid subordination of individual rights to group rights.

Kallen would have disapproved of the intensification of hostilities between different ethnic groups, for example, Slovaks and Irish versus blacks, or blacks who identified with the Arabs versus Jews. Yet, he would have been heartened by the revival in the late 1970s and early 1980s of a concern for democracy among many formerly disillusioned Americans and the latest generation of students. The ideal of American democracy, as formulated in the Declaration of Independence, he liked to call "the American Idea." To T. S. Eliot, an old friend and a lifelong critic of American values, Kallen in 1955 defended his championship of democracy and cultural pluralism as a passion and *mystique*. "As I see it, any concept is transvalued into a *mystique* whenever a person feels very strongly that it is important and precious not only for his own existence, but for all men's. The *mystique* of the American Idea [and cultural pluralism] differs from others in that it is a *mystique* of diversity, pluralism and equal liberty. . . . In the present crisis of human existence, I can't think of anything more indispensable to attaining global peace and freedom than such a *mystique* of democracy [and cultural pluralism]."[36]

A century ago, Walt Whitman wrote in his *Democratic Vistas* of the need for "Literatuses"—writers and thinkers—who would be the inspiration of the true democracy of distinctive individuals. Horace Kallen in our time was such a "Literatus"—creative image-maker and thinker. With Walt Whitman, he affirmed faith in the democratic idea and sought to inspire in all Americans the desire to create a "symphony of free, varied, mutually respecting men and women" of all the varied cultural, ethnic groups within American society.[37]

Notes

1. Horace M. Kallen, "Democracy versus the Melting Pot," *Nation* 100 (18, 25 February 1915): 190–94, 217–20; *Culture and Democracy in the United States* (New York, 1924); *Cultural Pluralism and the American Idea* (Philadelphia, 1956); *What I Believe and Why—Maybe* (New York, 1971), p. 129.

2. Michel de Crèvecoeur, *Letters from an American Farmer* (London, 1782), pp. 201–3; Oscar Handlin, ed., *Immigration as a Factor in American History* (Englewood Cliffs, N.J., 1959), pp. 146–49.

3. Edward Waldo Emerson and Waldo Emerson Forbes, eds., *Journals of Ralph Waldo Emerson*, 10 vols. (Boston, 1909–14), 7:115–16; Arthur Mann, ed., *Immigrants in American Life* (New York, 1968), pp. 139–40.

4. Israel Zangwill, *The Melting-Pot* (New York, 1909), pp. 37–38; John Higham, *Send These to Me* (New York, 1975), pp. 238–39; Mann, *Immigrants*, pp. 140–42.

5. Cf. Oscar Handlin, *The Uprooted*, 2d ed. (Boston, 1975), pp. 255–330; Richard D. Harper, *The Course of the Melting-Pot Idea to 1910* (New York, 1980),

pp. 233–335; John Higham, *Strangers in the Land*, (New Brunswick, N.J., 1955), pp. 68–193.

6. Kallen, *Culture and Democracy in the United States*, p. 124. For more light on Kallen's personal development and the relationship between his views on Zionism and cultural pluralism, see John Higham, *Send These to Me*, pp. 203–8; Horace M. Kallen, *What I Believe And Why—Maybe*, pp. 164–68; Milton R. Konvitz, "Horace Meyer Kallen (1882–1974): The Philosopher of the Hebraic-American Idea," *American Jewish Year Book 1974–75* (Philadelphia, 1974), pp. 55–78; Sara M. Schmidt, "Horace M. Kallen and the 'Americanization' of Zionism: In Memoriam," *American Jewish Archives* 28 (April 1976).

7. Perhaps an even better musical analogy for the role of ethnic groups in American society may be Ralph Ellison's felicitous description of jazz as "that embodiment of a superior democracy in which each individual cultivated his uniqueness yet did not clash with his neighbors." Cf. Louise M. Rosenblatt, "Whitman's Democratic Vistas and the New 'Ethnicity,' " *Yale Review* (Winter 1978): 187–202.

8. Horace M. Kallen Papers, American Jewish Archives, Cincinnati, Ohio, box 7, folder 14.

9. Horace M. Kallen, "Of the American Spirit," *The English Journal 35* (June 1946): 290.

10. Quoted in Sara Schmidt, "Horace M. Kallen," p. 60.

11. See Ronald Steel, *Walter Lippmann and the American Century* (Boston, 1980), pp. 186–96.

12. Cf. William N. Greenbaum, *The Idea of Cultural Pluralism in the United States, 1915–1975* (Ph.D. diss., Harvard University, 1978), pp. 92–93, 99–102.

13. Kallen, *Culture and Democracy in the United States*, pp. 92–97.

14. Cf. *Culture and Democracy in the United States*, pp. 114–17.

15. John Higham, *Send These to Me*, p. 208.

16. Kallen, "Alain Locke and Cultural Pluralism," in *What I Believe and Why—Maybe*, pp. 128–38. See also Kallen's essay, "Black Power and Education," idem, 101–14.

17. (Philadelphia, 1956).

18. Cf. Benjamin V. Cohen, "Human Rights under the United Nations Charter," in Sidney Ratner, ed. *Vision & Action* (New Brunswick, N.J., 1953), pp. 27–38. Benjamin Cohen, who played an important part in drafting this document, was a close friend of Horace Kallen's and an admirer of his philosophy of cultural pluralism.

19. Cf. letter from Kallen to Sidney Morgenbesser, 25 November 1958, American Jewish Archives, Cincinnati, Ohio.

20. Milton R. Konvitz, "Covenant of the Different, by the Different, for the Different," *Saturday Review*, 31 July 1971.

21. Randolph S. Bourne, "Trans-National America," *Atlantic Monthly* 118 (1916): 117; William N. Greenbaum, *The Idea of Cultural Pluralism*, p. 103.

22. Norman Hapgood, "The Jews and American Democracy," *Menorah Journal* 2 (1916): 202; an earlier essay by Hapgood was "The Future of the Jews in America," *Harper's Weekly* 61 (1915): 511–12.

23. John Dewey, "Nationalizing Education," National Education Association, *Addresses and Proceedings . . . 1916*, pp. 185–86.

24. John Higham, *Strangers in the Land*, pp. 250–52.

25. Gunnar Myrdal, *An American Dilemma*, 2 vols. (New York, 1944), 1:3–25, 92–97; 2:927–94. Cf. Thomas F. Gossett, *Race: The History of an Idea in America* (Dallas, 1963), pp. 339–459; John Higham, *Send These to Me*, pp. 198–218; Alexander Lesser, "Boas, Franz," *International Encyclopedia of the Social Sciences*, 15 vols. (1968), 2:99–110;

Stanford M. Lyman, *The Black American in Sociological Thought* (New York, 1972) pp. 27–70, 99–120; Fred H. Matthews, *Quest for an American Sociology* (Montreal, 1977), pp. 157–93.

26. (New York, 1947), pp. 59 ff.; John Higham, *Send These to Me*, pp. 221–23. In 1943 the U.S. Supreme Court took the position that the Constitution protects the freedom to be intellectually and spiritually diverse or even contrary. In 1947 several noted philosophers, e.g., Sidney Hook, Alain Locke, and Charles Morris, wrote essays in defense of cultural pluralism in *Freedom and Experience: Essays in Honor of Horace M. Kallen*, ed. Sidney Hook and Milton R. Konvitz (Ithaca, N.Y., 1947), pp. 3–114.

27. Ruby Jo Reeves Kennedy, "Single or Triple Melting-Pot?" *American Journal of Sociology*, 49 (1944): 332. Cf. her "Single or Triple Melting Pot?," idem. 58 (1952): 56–59.

28. (Garden City, N.Y., 1955).

29. (New York, 1964). See also his book, *Human Nature, Class and Ethnicity* (New York, 1978).

30. Milton Gordon, *Human Nature, Class and Ethnicity*, pp. 204–5.

31. (Cambridge, Mass., 1963), 2d ed. 1970.

32. (New York, 1971).

33. (Cambridge, Eng., 1976).

34. (University Park, Penn., 1977).

35. (New York, 1981).

36. Kallen to T. S. Eliot, 6 May 1955; H. M. Kallen Papers, American Jewish Archives, Cincinnati, Ohio. Quoted by permission of Dr. David Kallen.

37. L. M. Rosenblatt, "Whitman's Democratic Vistas," p. 204.

H. M. Kallen and the Hebraic Idea

MILTON R. KONVITZ

i

Ever since Heraclitus, thinkers have tended to discover that the basic principles in metaphysics, history, or culture are opposites that oppose and yet
maintain one another. The conflict is at the same time, to the eye that can
penetrate the surface appearances, a harmony. Day and night, winter and
summer, life and death, hot and cold—all polarities are happily brought into
harmony by Dike, Justice; yet the harmony is not destructive of the component opposites, each element is brought into measured change and into a
regulated discord. Thus in the intellectual history familiar to us, we learn of
such opposites as the Apollonian and the Dionysian, Rome and Jerusalem,
Apollo and Christ, the secular and the sacred, the City of God and the City
of Man.

Perhaps taking hints from Heine, Herder, and Lessing,[1] Matthew Arnold
in *Culture and Anarchy* (1869) introduced Hebraism and Hellenism as opposing forces or tendencies in English life, but like Heraclitus, he discovered
these opposites only because his fundamental motive was to synthesize them,
to combine them somehow into a holistic ideal to which each of these
polarities would make its proper, measured contribution. But what are these
opposites?

"The governing idea of Hellenism," wrote Arnold, "is *spontaneity of consciousness;* that of Hebraism, *strictness of conscience.*" Hellenism represents the
intellectual impulse, Hebraism the moral impulse. Hellenism is the effort to
see things as they really are, Hebraism is the effort "to win peace by self-
conquest." Each seeks the same end, that is, man's perfection or salvation, but
nothing can do away with their "ineffaceable difference"; for example, the

Hellenic quarrel with the body is that it and its desires hinder right thinking, while the Hebrew quarrel with them is that they interfere with right acting. Hellenism speaks of thinking clearly, seeing things in their essence and beauty; Hebraism speaks of becoming conscious of sin, of awakening to a sense of sin. The one stresses intelligence, the other obedience.[2]

To Arnold, neither Hellenism nor Hebraism was the law of total human development; each of them makes only contributions to that development. At times, however, it should be noted, Arnold speaks of Hellenism as the all-inclusive ideal, which takes into itself the Hebraic impulse for its contributions to the harmonious development of the totality of human powers.[3] The bent of Hellenism, he says, "is to follow, with flexible activity, the whole play of the universal order, to be apprehensive of missing any part of it, of sacrificing one part to another, to slip away from resting in this or that intimation of it, however capital." But more often Arnold speaks of Hellenism and Hebraism as opposing forces, to be harmonized, if possible, in what he calls *Culture*, which he sees as the harmonious expansion of *all* human powers.[4]

Arnold saw the Protestant Reformation as largely, though not exclusively, a flowering of Hebraism, and the Renaissance as a flowering of Hellenism. Puritanism was a reaction of Hebraism against Hellenism. It checked whatever Hellenic impulse there was in the Reformation.[5] The result has been, thought Arnold, that in his own day the main impulse of the strongest part of the English nation has been toward Hebraism. This, he thought, was a contravention of the "natural order." In the Preface to *Culture and Anarchy*, Arnold said,

> Now, and for us, it is a time to Hellenise, and to praise knowing; for we have Hebraised too much, and have over-valued doing.[6]

But the ideal of Hebraism, the ideal of righteousness, he went on to say, though it must be made to yield first place to the Hellenic impulse, such displacement must be only for the day. The nation must be prepared to restore Hebraism to the first rank tomorrow, for Hebraism is, he said,

> the discipline by which alone man is enabled to rescue his life from thralldom to the passing moment and to his bodily senses, to ennoble it, and to make it eternal.[7]

In his "Conclusion," Arnold looked toward the time when

> man's two great natural forces, Hebraism and Hellenism, will no longer be dissociated and rival, but will be a joint force of right thinking and strong doing to carry him towards perfection. This is what the lovers of culture may perhaps dare to augur for such a nation as ours.[8]

Although Arnold tried hard to perform a delicate balancing act with
Hebraism and Hellenism, he recognized that the idea of balancing was itself a
Hellenic ideal, for it was the Greeks whose ears were attuned to hear "*all* the
voices of human experience," that it was the Greeks who worked toward the
ideal of "a harmonious expansion of *all* the powers which make the worth of
human nature." It was among the Greeks that Arnold found the ideal of "a
human nature perfect on all sides." In idealizing the ancient Greeks, Matthew
Arnold was only one of a substantial number of Victorian writers—Benjamin
Jowett, Walter Pater, and George Grote were among the more notable ones—
who were influenced by the German Hellenists, for whom Goethe spoke
when he said:

The highest idea of man can be attained only through manysidedness,
liberality. The Greek was capable of this in his day. The European is still
capable of it.[9]

ii

In an essay on "Hebraism and Current Tendencies in Philosophy," which
Horace Kallen wrote in 1909 and which he included in his book *Judaism at
Bay*, published in 1932,[10] Kallen took over from Matthew Arnold the term
Hebraism but gave it a different and deeper meaning than it had for Arnold.
Arnold's use of the term, said Kallen, reflected a conventional, traditional
attitude, which falsified the essential nature of Hebraism. The difference
between the Hellenic and the Hebraic forms of thought and feeling, according to Kallen, was to be found, first of all, in their metaphysical insights. For
the Greek, the essence of reality was "structure, harmony, order immutable,
eternal." For the Greeks, the world was a composition—"a hierarchy of ideas,
or forms, each having an especial place in the whole; to them no thing could
be explained save by the larger unity to which it belonged." For the Greeks,
change is unreal and evil; what was from the beginning shall be at the end.
The great Greek tragedies, for example, portray the inexorable working of an
ancestral curse. Destiny is decisive. The Greek view of reality "is static and
structural." "To be Hellenic in philosophy is to deny that change is ultimately
real, to define any part by the 'whole' to which it belongs, to see the universe
as static."

When Hellenism is seen with eyes other than those of Matthew Arnold,
then, says Kallen, in truth Hellenism is not concerned with "seeing things as
they really are," "but with seeing things as they *ought to be*"—that is, ought to
be from the standpoint of the ancient Greeks.[11]

The Hebraic vision of reality, said Kallen, was the truer of the two, for it
saw "flux, mutation, imminence, disorder." The ancient Jews saw the world

as a flux, "in which events occurred freely according to no predetermined plan." The Hebraic world left room for change. Sin got punished, virtue was rewarded, but no one was immutably, unalterably a sinner, there was always room for atonement, for making a new life, a chance to be born again. There was no divine fiat that was unalterable. For the Hebraic man, the essence of reality was change. The Hebraic view was "dynamic and functional."[12]

For the ancient Jew, evil was real—it had an undeniable reality, like the stone that Samual Johnson kicked to refute Bishop Berkeley's idealism. He saw a world in which things were missing, where it was necessary to strain to win a foothold, a thing that one could possess. To him, the great virtues were faith, hope and charity—qualities that one needed to exist and to make one's way in a menacing environment.

The Hellenic mind, however, was preoccupied with the ordering of goodness—not a struggle to remove or reduce evil, but to so manipulate the pieces that make for goodness that the best order would result. The most representative Hellenic book is Plato's *Republic*, in which each of the chief virtues fits into a resultant harmony, while the most representative Hebraic book is Job. The constrast is between "nothing too much" and Job's cry, "I know that He will slay me; nevertheless will I maintain my ways before Him." Plato is "bothered by no protean environment ominous with evil; it needs only the ordering of goodness." Job, on the other hand, "represents the invincible loyalty of life to itself, in the face of overwhelming odds." But the slaying is not inevitable; for

> The very act of maintaining one's ways may render the slaying impossible. To belive in life in the face of death, to believe in goodness in the face of evil, to hope for better times to come, to work at bringing them about— that is Hebraism. Whether Biblical or Talmudic, that is the inner history of Jews, from the beginning to the present day—an optimistic struggle against overwhelming odds. That is Hebraism, but it is the Hebraism, not of childhood and innocence; it is the Hebraism of old age and experience. It is a vision of the world that has been tested in the furnace and come out clean.[13]

Kallen saw in the philosophy of pragmatism, and in the thought of William James and Henri Bergson, a rehabilitation of the Hebraic vision of reality. James defined a thing by what it does. Ideas are true if they lead prosperously, if they have genuine survival value, if they endure, if they work in the flux of things. Man's attitude must be "melioristic." Kallen interpreted James as saying:

> The world is all conflict; it contains evil, it is full of menace and danger. But these are not eternal. Man is genuinely free, he can change his world and himself for the better. He can ameliorate by his very faith. In a universe rich with actual contingencies, faith and works even of so small an

item as man, may be and often are, pregnant with tremendous human and even cosmic consequences. You are, therefore, entitled to believe at your own risk, and since the world is in flux, the mere existence of that belief may be just the one needed factor to make its object real. Nothing is eternally damned, nothing eternally saved; the contributing value to the validity of your beliefs, to the strength of your life, is as much yourself as the environment to which you must adapt yourself. But this is only the modern way of asserting in an unfortuitous environment "I know that He will slay me, nevertheless will I maintain my ways before Him."[14]

Kallen saw in Bergson "the most adequate exponent of this tested and purified philosophic Hebraism." Bergson saw reality, not in ideas, but as a moving act. Ideas fail to give the thickness, the richness, and above all the motion of reality. The ideas are static and dead, they are "mere instances, mere appearances of the propulsive flux of the universe, of its *élan vital*." It is only in *doing* that one gets at the *élan vital* of things and really knows and possesses them as they are.[15]

Now this, Kallen thought, was exactly the opposite of the Hellenic view, which found reality only in the static idea, the eternal and immutable structure of things. For Bergson, change and not immutability was real. Such a finding, in which the dynamic is real and the fixed is mere appearance, "is," said Kallen, "the essential finding of Hebraism."[16]

iii

This Hebraic vision, however, allowed itself to be supplanted by the intellectualism of the Greeks. Its innocent and unsophisticated feelings for the living, dynamic demands of life gave place to Hellenism as soon as Jewish thinkers began to think metaphysically; for to think philosophically was to Hellenize. The history of the philosophy of Jewish thinkers, as that of the whole of Christian thought, "is the history of an attempt to subordinate the prophets to Plato, revelation to Aristotle. From Philo to Mendelssohn, as from Augustine to Hegel, the attempt has been to make the dynamic and functional character of the universe an aspect, a mere appearance of the static and structural, to explain the part by the whole, mutation by identity." Philo saw in the teachings of the Torah the eternal ideas of Plato. For Jewish, as for Christian, philosophy, the God of Abraham, Isaac, and Jacob was replaced by the God of the philosophers who were Hellenists and not Hebraists in their metaphysical presuppositions. Contrary to what Matthew Arnold thought, Hebraism never dominated the thought of European life anywhere near the degree to which Hellenism dominated it.[17]

In other essays that he published in the first and second decades of the twentieth century, Kallen castigated Reform Judaism for having allowed itself to become thoroughly Hellenized. Denying its particularity and stressing its universal teachings, Reform Judaism, Kallen maintained, emptied itself of the most precious elements of the Hebraic inheritance. For, he said, "Mere universals are empty, futile, impotent, nugatory. The law of gravitation never did anybody either harm or good; a particular falling stone, a concrete moving train, has infinite capacity for both."[18]

In his criticism of Reform Judaism, as it developed in the early years of this century, Kallen often used phrases that would suggest a sympathy with nominalism or logical realism.

> Particularity, as opposed to universality, is the essence of life and power. The most universal thing is the deadest.
> To harp on the "universality" of Judaism, therefore, is to insist that it is futile, dead, or moribund; . . . Hebraism is a life and not a tradition; . . . a spirit, a concrete and particular mode of behavior, not a formula.[19]

Hebraism and Judaism, he said, "are growing and changing things, expressions of a palpable vitality, not dead unalterable 'universals.'" Contrary to the claims of the early spokesmen for Reform Judaism in the United States, Kallen maintained that

> What really destroys the Jews is what "universalizes" them, what empties their life of distinctive particular content and substitutes void phrases to be filled with any meaning the social and religious fashion of the day casts up.[20]

Precisely because Hebraism was particularistic, and not universalistic in its metaphysical and general philosophical tendencies and forces, it could easily change to accommodate the Jewish people to the demands of life. Its essence was plastic, malleable, fluid. It seems to have contained, wrote Kallen, "some labile principle which makes its basic teaching far less needy of revision than other religions. Baldly, this principle may be indicated by the words *naturalism* and *moralism*. These qualities make Jewish religion compatible with any phase of science and accommodating to every pressing human need."[21]

iv

Kallen used the term *Hebraism* rather than *Judaism* in order to keep what he thought of as the essential elements of the Jewish way of life and thought free of any element of religion in its more restrictive sense of the supernatural. He therefore liked to think of himself as a *Hebraist* rather than, to use his term, a *Judaist*. But he was not altogether consistent in this usage; there were times when he used the term *Judaism* in the same sense in which he used the term

Hebraism, and sometimes he spoke of both as if they were consistent with each other. Kallen could do this because he saw essential elements of Hebraism in Judaism. For example, Hebraism is not abstractly speculative; it is empirical and seeks experience directly. Well, so is Judaism. "The knowledge of God and his laws . . . was to be attained," he wrote, "*empirically and directly*, by no intermediaries, through a study of his manifestations. As Jehuda Halevi insists again and again: at Sinai God was immediately manifest to all the people, and his Torah is only the form of this natural manifestation. Descriptions of his character and desires consequently will vary with the occasion. They will always be empirical and often contradictory."[22] The contradictions are numerous and manifest—God is both personal and impersonal, knowable and unknowable, in the world and out of it, the source of goodness and the source of evil. But the one quality that remains the same is the "*efficacy, energy, life,* which the conflicting things have." Indeed, even the Torah itself *changes*. "Its words are fruitful and multiply." For the Torah consists not only of the first five books of Moses, but also of the writings of the prophets and the books of wisdom, "*the whole recorded life* of the Jewish people—in a word, of the wisdom gleaned through experience with the world."[23]

Kallen saw in Judaism the extraordinary union of naturalism with moralism. While other religions were supernatural even when moralistic, for Judaism existence, life, "is a good here and now." In Judaism there was no belief in original sin, in a Fall. "The rewards and punishments of conduct are here and now woven into the warp and woof of nature herself. *The moral order is not a supernatural order, the moral order is a natural order.* Incommensurate though God and man are, there is a directive preference *in* the universe, a 'something not ourselves which makes for righteousness,' which we feel and can obey, and must obey if we desire prosperity, and length of days. Whatever man's aim, man's *business* is not salvation; man's business is *righteousness*—'to do justice, and love mercy, and walk humbly with thy Lord.' Life on earth is not something to escape from. Life on earth is something to enjoy. It is obedience to the law, of course, but the law is not negative. The law is positive. It enjoins action, not abstinence."[24]

Kallen rejected the antinomism of Christianity. Society, he argued, grows and fructifies by interpretation of law that harmonizes the legal order with new situations. Indeed, the adequacy of a people's social sense may be measured by its legal tradition. Legalism, thus, means that Judaism could be and is progressive, "that it contains the principle of growth within itself." Legalism in detail results in moralism in the mass.

And because *moralism* is positive, social, and active, as opposed to *salvationism*, which is negative, private and passive, Judaism carries with it a joy of life that the rabbis called the "joy of the law." Judaism, consequently, as a corporate ethical tradition, has no conflict with the vision of human life enjoined by science.[25]

v

In a remarkable essay written in 1911, Kallen stated that the whole of the life of the Jews was best designated as Hebraism, while Judaism should be seen as only a special aspect of that life, namely, that "which comprises the sentiments, theories, doctrines and practices which relate to God."[26] When compared with other Western religions, Kallen found Judaism to be "overwhelmingly integrative and comprehensive"; still, it was not identical with the whole of life, and hence was not the most adequate expression of that life. The spirit of the life of the Jews, he thought, could best be conveyed by the term *Hebraism*.

But Kallen, while definitely not a supernaturalist and often an outspoken anticlerical, did not denigrate Judaism, for he perceived in Judaism much of the spirit of Hebraism. Judaism, for him, was naturalistic and realistic rather than supernaturalistic and salvational. The resemblance between naturalism and what is dominant in historic Judaism, he wrote, is striking. God has no specific image in Judaism; yet His manifestations are utterly of this world and empirical. "He shows himself as fire, as thundercloud, as storm, as the creator of monsters, as a man. . . ." In Job, He takes shapes that change and perish, though He remains. In that book, which Kallen considered the profoundest of all biblical texts, God

> is represented as dealing out indifferently good and evil, as having that absolute justice of indifference, of working out his purposes without reference to any of his particular creatures—simply the impartial *life* of all of them. God, according to the Book of Job, is his manifestations, both immanent and transcendent, different from them all as the whole is different from the part, but not otherwise; not different, as in the supernatural conceptions of him, by *existing apart*.[27]

Between Reform Judaism and Orthodoxy, Kallen saw much more in the latter that he favored; for he saw Orthodoxy as a way of life, "not as a collection of eviscerated doctrine and apologetic." That Orthodoxy was "suffused with much superstition and nonsense is," he said, "of course true." However,

> The significant thing is that nowhere else in western religions are the superstition and nonsense so little capable of withstanding science and sense. These penetrate with extraordinary ease into the very ritual and corporate life of the Jewish masses. The reason is that Judaism is so largely and literally a *mode of life*. And the principle of life is *change*, and change for the sake of life. From this it is that the other generic quality of Judaism, its *moralism*, derives.[28]

For Judaism, said Kallen, morality and things of the spirit are natural facts, which are to be empirically described and empirically understood. Reading the Hebrew Scriptures, especially the book of Job, and yet uncannily echoing Emerson's "Compensation," Kallen wrote:

> It requires no miracle to exhibit the moralism of the universe, creative, infinite, inscrutable though it be. Man knows it immediately, . . . and verifies his knowledge pragmatically. Nature and spirit, hence, are not alien, they are one, and the science that describes the one characterizes the other.[29]

His conclusion, not surprisingly, puts Judaism at the center of Hebraism. "Even though Judaism is a revealed religion," he wrote, "and thus in logic and method alien to the scientific point of view, what it reveals is itself so indeterminate, so much of the essence of change, that it remains, I think, truer to the spirit of positive knowledge and possesses consequently a greater capacity for endurance and for growth."[30]

vi

In his later years, Kallen tended to speak of himself as a secularist rather than as a Hebraist. I think that there were several reasons for this change. One reason was that the Roman Catholic hierarchy in the United States had begun a vigorous and sustained attack on what they called materialism and secularism. He saw in this campaign a declaration of war against many of the things that meant most to him—pragmatism, pluralism, naturalism, the scientific method, humanism, liberalism—many of the things and values that he had identified previously as Hebraism. In defending secularism, therefore, Kallen was, at least in large part, responding to the attacks by the Roman Catholic Church. A second reason, perhaps, is that he had come to realize that the term *Hebraism*, in the senses in which he had used it, had not taken hold in the way other terms that he had used became part of the public domain, like *cultural pluralism*, the *orchestration of differences*, the *right to be different*. *Hebraism* still suggested the essay by Matthew Arnold rather than the articles and books by Horace Kallen. A final reason, again only perhaps, since Kallen himself never explained the change, is that he was addressing the larger public rather than the Jewish community when he was speaking of secularism, and there would be fewer historical and mental obstacles to overcome than if he were to speak of Hebraism.

But there can be little if any doubt that to Horace Kallen secularism was essentially the same as Hebraism. In his essay on "Secularism as the Common Religion of a Free Society,"[31] he identifies other-worldly religions as having articles of faith that claim to be eternal, universal, and infallibly true, and that rely on a method that is dogmatic and dialectical. Their logic is that of a closed system. On the other hand, worldly religions have articles of faith

that are hypotheses which are ever undergoing tests for validation by consequences, and that are open to change in the light of consequences. They
have a logic of exploration and discovery. Other-worldly religions make their
bets on a future that they believe is certain and guaranteed, while a worldly
religion makes its bets believing that the future is by no means a sure thing.
Countless times Kallen quoted in his writings the cry of Job:

> I have no hope. I know that He will slay me. Nevertheless will I maintain
> my ways before Him. Mine integrity hold I fast and will not let go.

The essence of wisdom, he thought, is to see one's life as a "struggle to keep
on struggling," and to bet on the struggler over the event.

This essentially is how Kallen read Jewish history, the Jewish spirit. This
is how he read the Hebrew Scriptures and the other repositories of Jewish
thought and actions—all in the light of the Book of Job, which to him was the
essential expression of life and the spirit he called Hebraism.

Now in retrospect I wonder if it had not been better and wiser for Kallen to
have used the term *Judaism;* for his *Hebraism*—and his secularism, too—is a
poor, scanty thing when not interpreted in the light of Kallen's understanding
of the Jewish ethos, of Jewish history, Jewish thought and life—all of which,
and more, can be comprehended in the term *Judaism*. There are, as Kallen
himself noted, many Judaisms. According to the Jewish tradition, the Deca-
logue when spoken at Sinai was heard as if it had been spoken in the seventy
languages that men spoke. The Talmud notes that a great rabbi can learn even
from a learned apostate, like Elisha ben Abuyah; it is, said Rabbi Meier, like
eating a pomegranate, you drink the juice and throw away the seeds. "Turn it
around, turn it around," the rabbis taught, "for everything is in it." Who is
there who has the authority to define Judaism for all Jews and for all time? It
is well-nigh indefinable, but that is hardly an overriding objection; for
Hebraism, too, is ultimately indefinable; and so are the great, tantalizing
terms like Justice, Beauty, Goodness, Truth, Americanism, Christianity, and
countless other terms that we do not hesitate to use.

I wonder, too, if Kallen, like Matthew Arnold before him, did not overdo
the difference between Hellenism and Hebraism. C. P. Snow, who knew
something about the separation between two cultures, wrote that "the
number 2 is a very dangerous number: that is why the dialectic is a dangerous
process. Attempts to divide anything into two ought to be regarded with
much suspicion."[32] In an essay about his own intellectual development that
Horace Kallen wrote toward the end of his life, he said:

> What I learned and became converted to is the philosophic faith I have
> been confessing, reasoning about, and trying to give effect in words and
> works these fifty years. It identifies me as a libertarian who had been a

determinist, a temporalist who had been an eternalist, an individualist and nominalist who had been a universalist, a pluralist who had been a monist, without being alienated from what he had been. The sum of it—a Spinozist who became a pragmatist.[33]

But I am afraid he often *was* alienated from what he had been. There ought to be room in one's philosophy for monism as well as for pluralism, for a universe as well as for a multiverse, for determinism as well as for indeterminacy or contingency, for both time and eternity, for both change and permanency. Kallen believed, with all his heart, in the possibility of orchestrating the different, but he did not always use this talent, of which he was a master. What, it should be asked, was so awful about the Hellenistic influence on Jewish thought? about Philo of Alexandria bringing together—orchestrating, if you please—Judaism with neo-Platonism? or about Maimonides bringing together Judaism with Aristotelianism? Hellenistic civilization, despite its name, was not founded on pure Hellenism. For Jews, it was a bringing of the holiness of Shem into the tents of Japheth. Judaism gave to the union at least as much as it took. In any case, it can now be doubted if, for the majority of modern Jews, the process is reversible. For most of us, Hellenism and Hebraism have become orchestrated. And Judaism has not been impoverished by the union. "To substitute the society of ideas for that of things is," wrote Santayana, "simply to live in the mind: it is to survey the world of existences in its truth and beauty rather than in its personal perspectives, or with practical urgency. It is the sole path of happiness for the intellectual man, because the intellectual man cannot be satisfied with a world of perpetual change, defeat, and imperfection." That is well said, but Kallen would quite rightly remind Santayana that after all we do live in a world in which there is change, there is defeat, there is imperfection. Yet I, listening to both philosophers, would respectfully yet firmly interject with the observation that the world and man's life reveal both aspects; or, if you like, both Hebraism and Hellenism.

In conclusion let it be said clearly that Horace Kallen will occupy a unique and significant place in the history of American Jewry, for he was the first Jewish scholar in a non-Jewish college or university, teaching non-Jewish subjects, who yet wrote and lectured on Judaism and Jewish interests, and identified himself with and worked for Jewish causes; and for some years he was not only the first but the only one who stood forth in the academic world as a Jew, and in the Jewish world as someone from the strange world of American academia. For a few years Felix Frankfurter shared the stage with him, but in 1921 Frankfurter's public role as Jew essentially ended. Morris Raphael Cohen moved into Jewish interests with the rise of Nazism. In 1933 he played a leading role in the founding of the Conference of Jewish Relations, and six years later in establishing *Jewish Social Studies.* Today the situation is, providentially, quite different; but we must remember, with reverence and gratitude, the pioneering role that Horace Kallen played with the utmost dignity, devotion, and wisdom.

Notes

1. David DeLaura, *Hebrew and Hellene in Victorian England* (Austin, Tex., 1969), 183–86, 166, 191, 204–5.

2. Matthew Arnold, *Culture and Anarchy, and Friendship's Garland* (New York, 1883), pp. 112–13.

3. Ibid., p. 112.

4. Ibid., pp. xiv, xxxviii, 196.

5. Ibid., p. 122.

6. Ibid., p. xlii.

7. Ibid.

8. Ibid., p. 200.

9. Cited in DeLaura, *Hebrew and Hellene*, p. 165.

10. Horace Kallen, *Judaism at Bay* (New York, 1932).

11. "Hebraism and Current Tendencies in Philosophy," (1909) in *Judaism at Bay*, pp. 7–15.

12. Ibid., p. 9.

13. Ibid., p. 13.

14. Ibid., p. 12.

15. Ibid., p. 14.

16. Ibid., p. 15.

17. Ibid., p. 10.

18. "On the Impact of Universal Judaism," in *Judaism at Bay*, p. 24.

19. Ibid.

20. "Judaism, Humanism, and Zionism," in *Judaism at Bay*, p. 39.

21. "Judaism and the Modern Point of View," in *Judaism at Bay*, p. 47.

22. Ibid., p. 50.

23. Ibid., pp. 50–51.

24. Ibid., p. 54.

25. Ibid., p. 55.

26. Ibid., p. 42.

27. Ibid., pp. 49–50.

28. Ibid., p. 53.

29. Ibid., p. 56.

30. Ibid.

31. "Secularism as the Common Religion of a Free Society," in H. Kallen, *What I Believe and Why—Maybe: Essays for the Modern World* (New York, 1971).

32. C. P. Snow, *The Two Cultures and the Scientific Revolution* (1959), p. 9.

33. "Secularism as the Common Religion," p. 166.

Horace M. Kallen: The Zionist Chapter

SARAH SCHMIDT

Horace M. Kallen was a philosopher, an educator, a "scientific humanist," an "aesthetic pragmatist," who since the early years of this century consistently addressed a wide range of problems of contemporary concern, often recognizing and confronting relevant issues decades before they came into national prominence. Kallen's interest in minority cultures, for example, originated as early as 1905 when he began first to think about *the right to be different* that later became *cultural pluralism;* his concern with the environment and problems of human survival went back to contacts he made during World War I; his attention to man as consumer to experiences he had with the labor movement during the twenties. "It takes about fifty years for an idea to break through and become vogue," Kallen told me in 1972. He was fortunate to have lived long enough to see his early concerns validated by time and to know that scholars and policymakers, as well as the general public, were using his concepts and contributions of years ago for their continuing interest and stimulation.

There was, however, another side to Horace Kallen's life, reflecting his position as a Jew living in America. "I have always regarded you as the foremost creative American Jewish thinker who demonstrates by actual example that it is possible to live with distinction synchronously in two civilizations," wrote Mordecai M. Kaplan to Kallen in 1952, on the occasion of Kallen's seventieth birthday. Kaplan's appraisal was correct, for Kallen was eminently successful in defining and living his life both as an American and as a Jew from his single philosophical perspective of Hebraism, the source, according to Kallen, of both cultures. Hebraism, "individualism . . . , the right to be oneself, the right to be different," allowed Kallen to perceive his "Jewish difference [to] be no less real, worthy and honorable than any other," and helped Kallen to overcome his "dumb anxiety over [his] Jewish identity" by "living and orchestrating it" with the principles of the American Idea, principles of individual liberty and freedom he spent a lifetime explaining and teaching.[1]

Kallen, born in Germany in 1882, came to the United States as a young child when, in 1887, his family emigrated to Boston. His father was an Orthodox rabbi and, paralleling the experience of many immigrant sons, Kallen found his new world alien from that of his father. By the time he was an adolescent Kallen had denied for himself any validity in the Jewish doctrine, discarding both its theological and ritual content. But in 1902, while Kallen was a student at Harvard, Professor Barrett Wendell, "a Tory Yankee with Puritan heritage," helped bring him back to an identification with the Jewish people, a need that had become pressing with Kallen's sense of difference and isolation at Harvard.[2]

In his later years Kallen liked to recall how Wendell had emphasized the role of the Old Testament in defining a certain perspective and way of life. "He [Wendell] showed how the Old Testament has affected the Puritan mind [and] traced the role of the Hebraic tradition in the development of the American character. . . . And so I developed the interest in what you might call the Hebraic, the secular, the non-Judaistic component of the entire heritage and that naturally linked with what I knew about Zionism, the Herzl movement."

When, however, Kallen "returned" to "Jewishness," it was a Jewishness quite different from that of his father. Kallen continued to reject what he called the Judaist component of Jewish tradition—the theology, rituals, laws, and regulations of Jewish observance. Instead, he identified with what he defined as the Hebraic past of the Jewish people, a Hebrew-Jewish way of thought that constitutes a culture and binds a people together. Zionism, a secular Hebraic ideal whose goal was the renationalization of the Jewish people, became for Kallen the means through which he could affirm the past he had nearly discarded and remain within the Jewish community. Essentially, then, Kallen adopted Zionism as a new way to interpret Judaism. The *Jewish Idea*, as it had originally come to him, had seemed the antithesis of the freedom and democracy implicit in the *American Idea*. After 1902, Kallen began to construe the Old Testament as the source of the American Idea, the basis of the Declaration of Independence and of the Bill of Rights. Instead of being the embodiment of the rituals of Jewish theology, the Old Testament became the catalyst that had encouraged the formation of a free society with notions of equal liberty to all individuals and to all groups, no matter how different. Zionism, an ideal that Kallen felt would help to create another state dedicated to these same concepts of freedom and equality, was, therefore, highly compatible with the American Idea. A Zionist, Jewish or non-Jewish, was an individual expressing in another mode dedication to American ideals;

this particularly held true, however, for Jewish-Americans, with their special attachment to the Old Testament and their longstanding committment to the humanistic values of liberty and justice for all.

It is important to emphasize here that Kallen's decision to become a Zionist was an entirely personal one, based on an abstract formulation and influenced neither by the Jewish community nor by the fledgling American Zionist movement. In fact, Kallen did not recall knowing about any Zionist organization in 1902; his awareness of Herzl went back to conversations in his father's home and in the synagogue when he was a child. Thus when Kallen later became active in the Zionist movement, his approach and stance were rather different from those whose Zionist motivation emerged from any one of several European Zionist traditions. Significantly, his formulation of Zionism was to appeal to most to other American intellectuals who had become alienated from Jewish tradition and who were searching for some other way to retain or regain ties to the Jewish community.

In 1906 Kallen came to the attention of the Federation of American Zionists, who invited him to give a paper at their annual convention. Preparation of "The Ethics of Zionism," an interpretation of the Zionist idea based on Aristotle's *Politics* and *Ethics*, caused Kallen to clarify his own nascent views on Zionism, and in it he began to develop a cohesive expression of his Zionist reasoning.[3]

He began by rejecting two traditional Zionist positions—that Zionism is a charity to help free the masses from anti-Semitic persecution, and that Zionism is the fulfillment of an age-old religious instinct. Instead he felt that Zionism needed a new rationale, one that could show that the Jews deserved to live as a separate people in a country of their own.

In a rather elaborate exposition, Kallen extended the Darwinian principle of survival of the fittest from the individual to the social group, and applied this principle to the history of the Jewish people. Longer than any other people of recorded history, the Jew had survived, remaining "masterful and ever assertive, . . . molding the Western soul and setting before him definite controlling ideas." Since, Kallen argued, the message of the Hebraic prophets continues to be valid, the Jewish "race" has an ethical right to maintain its selfhood. But to do so, it, like the other nations of the world, needed to have "permanent occupation of a definite territory." "People's individuality cannot receive its highest and most adequate expression under an alien environment," Kallen asserted.

He then turned to the role of the Jews, particularly those living in America. "In America our duty to Zion is out duty to our children. . . . For of all things, the realization of the race-self is the central thing." Kallen demonstrated also a "radical" streak by demanding that Jews be willing to fight for the justice of their cause.

Our duty is to Judaize the Jew. . . . We have to crush out the Marrano [secret Jew], chameleon [assimilationists], and spiritual mongrel [Jews who imitated non-Jewish ritual]; we have to assert the Israelite.[4]

In "The Ethics of Zionism" Kallen first wrote of the themes he was to develop further in later years—his emphasis on abstract reasoning rather than on tradition or sentiment in explaining the need for a Jewish state; his concern with the survival of the complex of culture he called Hebraism; his conception that "each man in the human family has the right to live and to give his life ideal expression"—an idea that was to develop into *cultural pluralism;* his stress on the need for self-respect on the part of American Jews, a need that Zionist affiliation would help to promote; his willingness to advocate self-assertion.

By chance, Solomon Schechter, renowned biblical scholar and president of the Jewish Theological Seminary of America, happened to hear Kallen read his paper. In later years Kallen recalled, "In that paper I automatically applied what I had learned in my courses . . . and while most of the auditors either couldn't make out what I was driving at or were opposed anyhow—it was foreign to them in many ways and it was militant—Schechter liked it."

Schechter's positive response to Kallen's Zionist formulations, at a time when the majority of his audience could not comprehend them, is worth noting, for it was predictive of events as they were to unfold some ten years later. But, in fact, Kallen was quite willing to ignore the lack of understanding on the part of most American Zionists who heard him at that time. For he was approaching Zionism as a new convert and his enthusiasm to communicate his personally realized conception of the relationship between Hebraism and the American Idea to as wide an audience as possible helped him to overlook those who neither understood nor had the background to agree with him.

By far the most important individual to have been influenced by Kallen's formulation of Zionism was the famous "people's attorney" of the American Progressive movement, Louis D. Brandeis. Though Kallen, while an undergraduate at Harvard, had met Brandeis and had developed a friendly relationship with him, he had not thought it relevant to bring up his own developing interest in Zionism. Brandeis, after all, was well known as an arch-typical American assimilationist, whose background included no formal religious observances, no Jewish nationalistic leanings, no racial-cultural interests. At several public occasions Brandeis had clearly enunciated his strongly held view that "habits of living or of thought which tend to keep alive difference of origin or to classify men according to their religious beliefs are inconsistent with the American ideal of brotherhood, and are disloyal."[5]

In 1913, however, hearing that Brandeis had expressed some interest in

Zionism, Kallen sat down to write him something of his own Zionist philosophy. "In Palestine we aim at a new state and a happier social order. . . . I
venture . . . to suggest [that you] consider the general problems of agricultural and industrial organization as Zionism has to face them, and to
formulate such a plan as will . . . [address] social justice as well as economic
gain. . . ."

Kallen also sent Brandeis a copy of a paper he had written in 1910 in
response to rabbinical attacks aimed at Kallen's rejection of Reform Judaism. In
that paper Kallen had hinted at some of the cultural pluralist rationale he was
later to make more explicit, using phrases like "culture . . . constitutes a
harmony . . . to which each [nation] contributes its unique tone," and "what
really destroys the Jews is what 'universalizes' them, what empties their life of
distinctive particular content."[6]

Several months later, in response to a request from Brandeis for an elaboration of his views, Kallen framed a memorandum, "The International Aspects
of Zionism." He presented this paper to Brandeis on an overnight boat trip
they took together to attend an "Extraordinary Conference of Representatives
of American Zionists," a meeting at which Brandeis, overcoming his concerns about dual loyalty, allowed himself to accept the chairmanship of the
Provisional Executive Committee, which would guide Zionist affairs during
the period of the First World War.

The initial section of Kallen's memorandum incorporated much of his
Zionist thinking. In it he argued that a new Jewish nation would revive the
Jewish culture and, though presenting the viewpoints of both the so-called
practical and political Zionists, concluded that "there can be no 'cultural
centre' without a political centre." He rejected the idea of Zionism as philanthropy, stressing that Palestine must become free from dependence on
charity in order for Jews to express their "ethnic nationality" freely and
autonomously. He showed how the American Jewish community was in
danger of dying without a Jewish national homeland with which it could
identify. He reiterated the thoughts he had expressed in a 1913 speech before
a convention of the Boston Order Knights of Zion.

> . . . As the individual Jew makes the best of himself as a citizen of the
> United States . . . only by developing and expressing what is best in his
> nature as a Jew freely and autonomously, so the Jewish people can give
> their best to civilization . . . only by expressing the nature of the race freely
> and autonomously. We must seek, therefore, first and foremost, this auton-
> omy of the Jewish State among the states of the world. . . .[7]

Kallen's thoughts were new to Brandeis, for most of them were not part of
the standard European Zionist ideology with which he might have been
familiar. Their effect on Brandeis and their contribution to Brandeis's deci-

sion to move from a somewhat lukewarm sympathy for the aspiration for a Jewish State to his assumption of the active leadership of the entire American Zionist movement can be only a matter of historical conjecture. But the fact that shortly thereafter Brandeis was to repeat almost verbatim many of Kallen's ideas demonstrates, with certainty, that they made a significant impression on him.

Indeed, an analysis of the arguments for Zionism that Brandeis so forcefully and consistently brought before the American people after 1914 shows that they bear, almost phrase by phrase, an uncanny similarity to the Zionist statements of Horace Kallen.[8] By 1915, for example, Brandeis, the former apostle of assimilation, was saying that "the new nationalism adopted by America proclaims that each race or people, like each individual, has the right and duty to develop." Negating his earlier concepts of dual loyalties, Brandeis now suggested that American Jews, free from civil or political disability, were best fit to lead the struggle to found a Jewish nation that shared America's "fundamental law" of the brotherhood of man as well as "America's insistent demand" for social justice. Like Kallen some ten years earlier, Zionism as Americanism had become Brandeis's way to ease his identity conflicts as an American Jew.

The influence of Kallen's ideas, reflected in Brandeis's statements, went even further, however. As Kallen indicated to me two years before he died:

> Now Brandeis took up the ideas . . . and after he identified himself with the Zionist movement . . . he presented in his own language the essential ideas. And in presenting those ideas, the conflicts that he had imagined between Zionism and Americanism . . . were simply nullified. Now that gave Zionism publicly a philosophical status in terms of what you might call the American faith, and gave it a public force that it couldn't possibly have had from me alone.

Kallen, through Brandeis, thus became the philosopher of an Americanized Zionism, the intellectual who worked behind the scenes with a leader who was to remake the Zionist movement in America. From 1914 until 1921, when a major dispute between the American Zionist leaders and their European counterparts over their differing conceptions of Zionism forced Brandeis and Kallen to leave the Zionist movement, Brandeis relied on Kallen in many ways. Kallen, like Brandeis, an advocate of "progressive" reform in American life, helped to formulate and to implement plans for efficient reform of the American Zionist organization; his fertile mind originated many of the practical ideas that Brandeis and others used as a basis for action in the Jewish community; he became a "missionary" trying to convert both Jews and non-Jews to the Zionist cause; he was, for quite some time, the sole American link with important Zionist activity in Great Britain.[9] But perhaps his single most lasting contribution to American Zionism was his preparation of the plans that American Zionists used, down to the last detail, as the basis for their vision of a newly constructed Jewish State.

In August 1914, in "The International Aspects of Zionism," the memorandum that Kallen had submitted to Brandeis on their way to the formation meeting of the Provisional Executive Committee, Kallen had included an outline of the utopia he foresaw for Zion. The aim of the Zionist organization, as he saw it then, was to establish a state in which the government would facilitate the expression of the ethnic nationality of the Jewish people—their language, literature, religion, philosophy, art. He suggested, therefore, a centralized international organization to work out "a carefully reasoned plan for the central control of all practical activity in Palestine." This organization would have five divisions; (1) a ministry of public affairs to be in charge of "the consistent development of the settlement, the establishment of industries, etc."; (2) a ministry that would apply uniform laws, "so as to maintain the practice of democracy and to avoid economic and social injustice"; (3) a ministry to develop a system of national education from grade school to university; (4) a ministry of public health; and (5) a ministry to establish a Bureau of National Art.[10]

For some time the working out of the implications of this scheme occupied Kallen's mind. In April 1915 he wrote of it to Brandeis and shortly thereafter attempted to involve Felix Frankfurter more closely with the Zionist movement by sending him the following note:

> I meant what I said when I talked with you about considering a job as a director of a "Ministry of Interior. . . ."
> It seems to me that your particular job ought to be the consideration of the following things: (1) What are the economic and commercial assets of Palestine? (2) What is being done . . . to develop them? (3) How shall the work of development be organized so as to secure social justice and the ends of public happiness and safety? (4) How shall this be done so as to give all of our young people at one and the same time training in defense of their country . . . and positive services to the country for its development, i.e. can we really establish a "moral equivalent" for war?[11]

Though there is no record of any response by Frankfurter, Kallen's papers show that his concern with developing practical plans for the Jewish nation-to-be continued to be the focus of most of his efforts for the Zionist organization. It is not surprising, therefore, that in 1918, taking seriously what he construed to be the British promise in the Balfour Declaration (the statement viewing with favor the establishment in Palestine of a "National Home" for the Jewish people), Kallen began to formulate specific programs, along American Progressive reform lines, to ensure the economically and socially just development of Palestine.[12]

He began by writing to the leaders of the Zionist movement in both the

United States and England to remind them of their obligations to look beyond the victory of the moment toward the problems of the future. To Alfred Zimmern, an English political scientist and authority on international relations, who was his closest contact in Great Britain, he noted, "I am sure that an experiment in social justice in Palestine, because of the limitation of the area, the concreteness of its problems, is much more likely to be significant . . . than anything that can happen in Russia for generations. . . ."[13] And, "I want as nearly as possible to think out a modus vivendi which will lead to an ultimate United States of Asia Minor, involving the Jews, Arabs, Armenians, etc., under international or British guarantee." Somewhat presciently he warned Brandeis, "I am frank to say that I am disturbed by the possibility that the [Palestinian] colonies may be restored and new undertakings begun without regard to the fundamentals of economic organization that would insure a real democracy. . . . I hope that we may have a frank consideration by the leadership of what is involved, and the definition of a progressively democratic economic program. Unless we do this, we shall saddle ourselves at once with a labor-problem and a workman's party which will shame us, and rightly."[14]

Though he was reluctant to contact Chaim Weizmann, leader of the British Zionists, directly, he finally did so in January 1918. He urged Weizmann to initiate serious discussions "on methods which will establish fundamental economic, as well as political democracy in our new homeland." In a strong allusion to his own definition of Zionism, Kallen concluded, "This [economic and political democracy] is primarily within the original tradition of our people and its reformulation in contemporary terms will not break but help the continuity of our history."[15]

Kallen did not wait, however, for others to act. In the spring of 1918 he published his "Constitutional Foundations of the New Zion," a description of the structure of the new "commonwealth" as Kallen envisioned it. Kallen had been influenced by Robert Owen, a British socialist of the early nineteenth century, who held that the key to human progress was in economic, not political, reform. Owen wished to make the existence of the private landowner and capitalist impossible; his socialism consisted of a reorganization of society on the basis of public property, that is, common ownership of the land and of the machinery of wealth production, as well as communal supervision of the distribution and production of all material goods. Moreover, Owen devised a form of child-centered education that would teach a new generation to feel comfortable in a society where a sense of trust would replace the competitive drive.

Kallen felt that plans such as Owen's were especially appropriate for the reconstruction of Palestine, where the Jews would have a great advantage in building, from the beginning, a "genuine creative democracy." By democracy Kallen had come to mean the "liberation, encouragement and differences among men, the increase of human individuality and spontaneity and hence of human cooperation."[16] The constitutional foundations he proposed were designed to bring the new state to this level of democracy.

Kallen proceeded to compare the function of the state to that of a traffic policeman: "it is to keep the ways of life open to the free movement toward the expression and fulfillment of their natural capacities by individuals and groups." Its most important role would be the abolition of private ownership and "privilege of any sort," and, even more important, to prevent them from arising in the first place.[17]

To this end, Kallen made several concrete suggestions. He felt that there should be public ownership of "the whole Jewish land,"[18] as well as of all natural resources, means of transportation and communication. Individuals or groups undertaking any operation using the land or its resources would become the tenants of the state, and leases would terminate, as in ancient Israel's "Year of the Jubilee," every fifty years. No tax system would be needed, for the public treasury would accrue enough funds from these leases to finance the needs of the state. Every industrial or agrarian organization would have to be a cooperative company, in which all its members would share alike; each cooperative unit would join with others to form a national association of the industry or profession, charged with responsibility for its own progress.

Kallen saw only two fundamental functions for the state—public defense and education. He defined medicine as "public defense against disease," and suggested that all doctors, hospitals, and schools of medicine be socialized. The other line of public defense would be against crime and war. Here Kallen recommended the creation of a state's militia to consist of "young men and young women of whose education this work will be a part." He also proposed universal schooling through college, to be financed by the state; part of each school year would be devoted to police and military training and to service on public works.[19]

These propositions do not seem particularly shocking today. As a matter of fact, the State of Israel has incorporated almost all of them. But in the context of post–World War I Zionist thought, Kallen's ideas were seen as revolutionary. The English Zionists, for example, feared Kallen's leap in accepting the premise of a State, and criticized his ideas for being "too little Jewish." Nevertheless, Kallen defended his proposals. "I do not think we ought to bother about 'Jewish point of view and Jewish policies,'" he wrote to Jacob deHaas, a leader of the Zionist Organization of America. "Jews working together will have these automatically. . . ."[20] Honesty and tactics, he felt, required the American Zionist movement, his audience for the "Constitutional Foundations," to "stand publicy by the 'great program.'"[21]

Indeed, Kallen and the American Progressive oriented Zionists, whose mentor he had become, went even further with plans for a Jewish State.

Kallen's draft, "A Memorandum on the Principles of the Jewish Commonwealth in Palestine," formed the basis of the so-called Pittsburgh Program, a
series of seven principles that the delegates to the 1918 convention of the
newly formed Zionist Organization of America adopted as its credo. Following along the lines both of Kallen's "Memorandum" and "Constitutional
Foundations," the Pittsburgh Program stressed political and civil equality for
all inhabitants of Palestine irrespective of race, sex, or faith; ownership and
control of the land and of all natural resources and public utilities "by the
whole people"; application of the cooperative principle in the organization of
all agricultural and industrial undertakings; a fiscal policy to protect the
people from the evils of land speculation; and a system of free public instruction, in the Hebrew language, for all grades of instruction.

   To Kallen and his followers, the Pittsburgh Program, based as it was on
Kallen's ideals of pluralism, Hebraism, and the American Idea, represented
their crowning achievement in expressing their faith and vision in reordering
Palestine as a model Jewish democratic nationality. Like many of Kallen's
ideas, however, the Jewish masses and the leaders of Zionist movements in
countries other than the United States never understood or accepted it. The
American Yiddish press of the period, for example, simply ignored it, and
the American Zionists of European background who, by their vote of no
confidence, forced Brandeis to resign from the Zionist movement in 1921,
repudiated it by implication.

   Kallen's scheme for Palestine, however, remained until the day he died his
ideal of what the Jewish nation might have become. Looking backward, he
recalled:

> I was a radical, in the sense that I wanted action. I wasn't prudent—a
> radical in that sense, and in that sense perhaps also impractical, because the
> commonwealth notion was regarded, perhaps rightly, as an impractical
> notion. Although I say perhaps rightly, I feel, actually, wrongly. I think if
> we had started with it [the Pittsburgh Program] the whole history of the
> movement and its achievment might have been very different. But then,
> you know, "what might have been. . . ."[22]

Between 1918 and 1921, after it became clear that the Pittsburgh Program
was not to have the effect on the Zionist movement and on the restructuring
of Palestine that Kallen had hoped for, he found himself and his group of
followers increasingly pushed to the periphery of both worldwide and American Zionist affairs. The European Zionists and the American Zionists of
recent European origin who supported them rejected the program of economic rehabilitation and democratic development that Kallen and Brandeis
continued to propose. Instead, the Europeans insisted that their newly organized Zionist Commission take charge of the Jewish community in Palestine—control the schools, organize the community politically and socially,

direct colonization and land reclamation, and regulate immigration. Kallen refused to be swayed from his convictions. "The time for a straightforward and clean-cut stand on fundamental principles is at hand," he wrote to the Executive Committee of the Zionist Organization of America. "If it must be American Zionism against the world, then let it be so. . . ."[23] This attitude caused Kallen and his principles to lose the struggle for the control of the American Zionist organization. In 1921 the majority of delegates to the Zionist Organization of America convention failed to return a vote of confidence in the American administration; thereupon Kallen and those whose visión of Zionism he had influenced resigned from the movement. On 7 June 1921, the Kallen/Brandeis era in American Zionism was over.[24]

One of the most poignant ironies of Kallen's rejection by the American Zionist movement was that the cultural pluralist argument he had formulated had been the theoretical underpinning that gave Jewish immigrants to America the freedom to join the Zionist movement without worrying about being accused of dual loyalties. Most American Jews, recent immigrants similar to the majority of the delegates to the 1921 convention, had been reluctant to identify themselves as Zionists before 1914, when Brandeis became the Zionist chairman. It had seemed, then, un-American and unpatriotic. The Americanized Zionism of Kallen and of Brandeis had made membership in the Zionist organization respectable. Cultural pluralism implied that being a hyphenated American was better than being an assimilated, or "melted" one. Yet it was these new members of the Zionist organization, men and women of European background, who Kallen felt certain could be educated to his vision of Zionism as the real possibility for a better world through the application of intelligent planning, that found Kallen's approach to Zionism too American and, therefore, foreign to them. Kallen, who all his life had championed majority rule, now found himself a victim of it. The Zionist masses simply could not follow the Utopian vision of this "melioristic" intellectual whose unfamiliar ideas they had come to resent.

The year 1921, however, saw the publication of a book on which Kallen had been working since 1915. *Zionism and World Politics: A Study in History and Social Psychology* presents Kallen's opinions liberally mixed with a wealth of detail on the history of Zionism. It was and remains a storehouse of information about the international movement for Jewish nationalism from its origins in the Middle Ages until July 1921. Roughly half the book deals with the years after World War I and describes, with the intimacy of a close witness, the behind-the-scenes negotiations at the Versailles Peace Conference, the jockeying among the major powers for influence in the Middle East, and the politics involved in awarding the Mandate for Palestine to Great Britain. The next to last chapter, explicit in its expression of Kallen's own point of view, bears the title, "San Remo: The End of an Epoch."

Kallen called his final chapter "Vita Nuova?" To him, in 1921, this was what the promise of Zionism held out. Much of the chapter deals with Kallen's economic theories, and Kallen supplies additional, explicit details for making Palestine the equitable society he had wanted the Zionist movement to create. The question mark, however, is significant, for Kallen felt that few others recognized the opportunities that had opened up, almost overnight, in Palestine. Since Kallen had become disillusioned by 1921 in his attempts to influence the Zionist movement from within, "Vita Nuova?" is, in part, a public polemic to try to convince Zionists to assume new ways of thinking and of acting.

To some extent, "Vita Nuova?" represents the swan song of Kallen's work as a Zionist activist. The strong words he used expressed his despair accurately. "Here at last," he wrote, "is the salutation [validation of the Balfour Declaration by the San Remo Treaty] which has been the sustaining hope of the heart of Jewry through the bitter ages, challenging them to new life. Yet the manner in which they respond to it leaves room to doubt whether the attainment of this new life shall not become a process painful, lingering, and—disillusioning."[25]

In late 1921 Kallen's English friend Zimmern came to the United States for a lecture tour and spoke, among other places, at the banquet of the Harvard Menorah Society. Kallen introduced Zimmern; the words he used were the same he might have applied to himself: "Professor Zimmern is one of a little group of men who had faith in the flexibility and the goodness of human nature to believe that a better world could actually be made instead of grown; he believed in the power of intelligence and in the value of foresight. . . ."[26] Like Zimmern, Kallen remained optimistic, with faith in progress and a commitment to social change. He told me in 1972, "Learning means finding alternatives to that which has failed."

In the years after 1921 Kallen remained a Zionist, continuing to work for the creation of a Jewish State in the way he thought best. He circulated yet another memorandum proposing a new Zionist group, "The Palestine Cooperative Trading and Credit Company," which would raise money to foster economic undertakings in Palestine, with the aim of developing as many self-supporting Jewish settlements as possible. Brandeis picked up the idea and suggsted to several prominent—albeit non-Zionist—philanthropists that they devote themselves "to raising money and spending it in Palestine for productive purposes"—a proposal that at the time bore little fruit.[27]

But Kallen turned most of his energies away from the Zionist organization toward groups where he could more effectively express his concern for freedom and for social justice. "The Zionist situation didn't seem to me to offer any opportunities for usefulness," he recalled. "I would have been blocked doing my own thing and I'm not the kind of person who would do another person's thing."[28]

The decade that Kallen had spent in the service of the Zionist movement,

however, had been an important one. For a few bright years the Zionist
organization had pulsated with energy and with hope, in no small measure
due to Kallen's quiet influence in the places he felt it would do the most good.
His ideas helped to change the American Zionist movement from a small,
rather inefficiently managed group to one that grew rapidly in numbers,
financial resources, and influence. His approach to Zionism gave it a uniquely
American cast.

Americanized Zionism was ultimately to make several critical contributions to the American Jewish community. It offered to Westernized accultu-
rated Jews, for whom religious tradition seemed outmoded or sterile, an
alternative, secular way to preserve their Jewish identity. As Kallen had
suggested in his arguments for cultural pluralism, it gave American Jews an
outlet for their ethnic sentiment, allowing them to participate on equal terms
with other ethnic groups of the American pluralistic society. It became the
major factor in uniting the American Jewish community, thus helping to slow
down the rate of assimilation in an open society that encouraged it. But not
until after the tragic events of the 1930s and 1940s in Europe, and the
establishment of the State of Israel in 1948, did a new generation of accultu-
rated, more secure American Jews feel free to affiliate with an "Americanized"
Zionism. Ironically, it was the role that Kallen and Brandeis had outlined in
1921, that of fundraisers for the upbuilding of the Palestine community, that,
since 1948, American Zionists have followed as their own.

Ironically, also, it was Kallen's fate to have lived long enough to see the
creation of the Jewish "commonwealth," only to analyze it in 1958, with some
disappointment, as *Utopians at Bay*. Happily, he remained a meliorist whose
hope sprang eternal. When he was ninety-one years old he wrote:

> . . . [There are those] who think [of] Israel as the present phase of an
> ongoing struggle to embody a historic faith in present fact, [who] regard
> Israel as an ideal bet on a future of equal liberty and equal safety under law;
> but a bet which cannot be a sure thing and nevertheless must have the
> generous support of American Jews as Americans and also as Jews. . . .[29]

This was Horace Kallen's 1973 evaluation of the task of American Zionists.
That his own crucial role in "Americanizing" Zionism had gone un-
acknowledged for so long is an impressive tribute to his own modesty. But it
is well, also, that some instinct impelled him to preserve so carefully his
papers, so that we can finally accord him the recognition and credit he so
eminently deserves.

Notes

1. Harvard Class of 1903, 50th Annual Report (1953); Horace M. Kallen, "What I
Have Learned, Betting My Life," in *What I Believe and Why—Maybe* (New York, 1971),
pp. 170, 173.

2. For documentation of this, as well as biographical details in the paragraphs that follow, see my (unpublished) dissertation, "Horace M. Kallen and the Americanization of Zionism" (University of Maryland, 1973). Much of this biographic information comes from three lengthy interviews Kallen accorded me in 1972 and 1973 and from my personal correspondence with him in those years.

3. Kallen, "The Ethics of Zionism," *The Maccabean* 11 (August 1906): 61–71.

4. Ibid., pp. 62, 70, 71.

5. Much has been written about Brandeis's "conversion" to Zionism. For a presentation of many of these theories, as well as more complete substantiation relating to the Kallen-Brandeis connection, see Schmidt dissertation, especially chaps. 4 and 5.

6. Horace M. Kallen, "Judaism, Hebraism, Zionism," in *Judaism at Bay* (New York, 1932), pp. 37, 39.

7. Unpublished address marked "To the Convention Order Knights of Zion," 26 December 1913, in the Horace M. Kallen Collection, (KC-AJA), American Jewish Archives, Cincinnati, Ohio.

8. Sarah Schmidt, "The Zionist Conversion of Louis D. Brandeis," *Jewish Social Studies* 37 (January 1975): 18–34, presents a complete analysis of Brandeis's speeches and their use of Kallen's ideas and themes.

9. Details supporting these contentions are in Schmidt dissertation, chaps. 6–9.

10. Horace M. Kallen, "International Aspects of Zionism," KC-AJA. This unpublished memorandum is headed by a handwritten notation, "Copy submitted to Mr. Brandeis, August 19, 1914."

11. Kallen to Felix Frankfurter, 9 April 1915. KC-AJA.

12. Sarah Schmidt, "Horace M. Kallen and the 'Progressive' Reform of Zionism," *Midstream* 22 (December 1976): 14–23, explores further the influence of the Progressive movement on Kallen's Zionist ideas, as does Schmidt dissertation, chap. 10.

13. Kallen to Alfred Zimmern, 11 January 1918, KC-AJA.

14. Kallen to Louis Brandeis, 17 January 1918, KC-AJA.

15. Kallen to Chaim Weizmann, 17 January 1918, KC-AJA.

16. Horace M. Kallen, "Constitutional Foundations of the New Zion," *The Maccabean* 31 (April–May 1918): 99.

17. Ibid., 100.

18. Ibid., 127.

19. Ibid., 127–28.

20. Kallen to Jacob deHaas, 22 September 1918, KC-AJA.

21. Kallen to Stephen S. Wise, 20 October 1918, KC-AJA.

22. Interview with author, 9 August 1973.

23. Kallen to the Executive Committee, Zionist Organization of America, 11 March 1919, KC-AJA.

24. Schmidt dissertation, chap. 11, more fully delineates Kallen's final years as an active Zionist.

25. Horace M. Kallen, *Zionism and World Politics* (New York, 1921), p. 276.

26. Horace M. Kallen, unpublished address before the Harvard Menorah banquet, 12 December 1921. KC-AJA.

27. Horace M. Kallen, "Memorandum on the Necessary Contents of the Charter of the (proposed) Cooperative Trading and Credit Company," KC-AJA; Nathan Straus, Jr., to Kallen, 13 June 1921, KC-AJA.

28. Interview with author, 9 August 1973.

29. Horace M. Kallen, " 'Israel'—Its Impact," *The Workmen's Circle Call* (May–June 1973): 8.

Horace M. Kallen and John Dewey on Cultural Pluralism and Jewish Education

RONALD KRONISH

Horace M. Kallen, a philosopher and educator who became known for his theory of cultural pluralism, was an important link for American Jewish educators (in the first half of this century)—through his contacts with John Dewey and other American philosophers and intellectuals—to the general philosophical and academic community. Through his avowed secularism and scholarship, especially in the realm of philosophy, he attempted to bring Dewey's pragmatism, at least in spirit, into high-level discussions of Jewish education in this country.[1] Kallen's doctrine of cultural pluralism, whose underpinnings in both James and Dewey will be discussed below, was an important element in the framework for developing a new system of American Jewish education in keeping with twentieth-century democratic ideals. Moreover, Dewey's views on cultural pluralism, especially with reference to the Jewish group, were inspired by Kallen, and they provided useful support for Jewish educators who were arguing passionately for the importance of ethnic survival in democratic America.

A graduate of Harvard College, where he studied with George Santayana and William James, Kallen shunned the traditional Judaism of his childhood in favor of philosophy as his new faith. Yet, even after he completed his doctorate in philosophy and became a professor of philosophy, he never separated his profession from his daily life, blending his philosophical and humanistic concerns with his Jewish commitments and ideology into a unique point of view that he called Hebraism.[2] While Kallen demonstrated a wide range of interests and activities in Jewish and American life, he was first and foremost a philosopher. From his days as a student and teaching assistant at Harvard, he always considered himself a philosopher in the American pragmatist tradition. As one of the chief exemplars of radical empiricism in the modern era,[3] Kallen's commitments to religion, science, and democracy were interlinked. Even though he was not formally religious, he was always sympathetic to those elements in religion, traditional as well as liberal, that expressed attitudes toward life that he felt were compatible with the best insights of humanism and science. As a logical corollary of his naturalistic humanism, Kallen was a great believer in science and democracy. Along with his belief in the openness of diversity in democracy as a fundamental premise went Kallen's doctrine of cultural diversity, which understood democracy's uniqueness in its ability to orchestrate different ethnic and religious groups into a harmonious whole.

It was primarily as a social philosopher and social activist that Kallen encountered both the philosophy and person of John Dewey. Dewey was, without doubt, one of the leading philosophers and educators of the era, and his theories had a strong influence upon leading Jewish educators of the period.[4] Kallen and Dewey, coming out of a shared philosophical tradition of American pragmatism, found common ground in the concept of cultural pluralism, and this concept made a strong impact on theoreticians of Jewish education in the 1920s and 1930s. The dynamics of how Kallen understood Dewey, and how Dewey influenced Kallen's doctrine of cultural pluralism, and how together both these thinkers made an impact on Jewish education, will be explored here.

Kallen and Dewey

Kallen's ideas about religion, science, and democracy were very much a part of the *zeitgeist* of his day. When he joined the faculty of the New School for Social Research in 1919, at the age of thirty-six, he found himself privileged to be associated with like-minded colleagues, including Charles Beard, James Harvey Robinson, Thorstein Veblen, Alvin Johnson, and John Dewey. Previous to his coming to the New School, Kallen had already been in contact with Dewey. According to his own recollections, Kallen originally encountered Dewey at the first meeting of the American Philosophical Association·in Cambridge in 1905 or 1906 where Dewey was presenting a lecture on his version of instrumentalism.[5] Following his years at Harvard, when Kallen was at Wisconsin, he corresponded with Dewey off and on, sometimes about philosophical issues, and sometimes about common organizational concerns. Kallen recalled that "we had a kind of overlap of interest, and I, myself, was especially interested in civil rights, interests which led into the American Civil Liberties Union when it was formed and into the Consumer Co-operative Movement and so on. . . . It was natural to want to get Dewey to participate in all these, and he did."[6]

Until Kallen moved from Wisconsin to New York, his relationship with Dewey was mainly by correspondence, except on occasions when he came to New York to visit or teach. During the summer of 1917, Kallen taught at Columbia on Dewey's invitation, and during this time they became better acquainted.[7] Kallen was invited again by Dewey to give a course of lectures at Columbia in the spring of 1918. It was not until the founding of the New School, however, that Kallen began to have a continuing relationship with Dewey. He saw him often, in various connections. In 1927, after he returned from Europe, he organized a course at the New School on problems of freedom and invited Dewey to be one of the lecturers in the course.[8] Dewey accepted and gave a lecture on "Philosophies of Freedom."[9] They also published a book together, entitled *Freedom in the Modern World*, with Dewey writing one of the chapters. Kallen believed that the issue of freedom ought to be a central one for the academic community—in fact, "freedom was the primary concern in the whole development of the New School Idea and its contemporary bearings."[10]

From his contacts with Dewey in his Harvard and early New School days, through their opposition to Nazism in the 1930s, and their support of Bertrand Russell in the Russell Case in the 1940s, Kallen and Dewey collaborated on some of the most important philosophical and political issues of the period. At various times, Kallen joined with many others to pay tribute to Dewey on some of his birthday celebrations, especially Dewey's seventieth and ninetieth birthdays. In 1929, Kallen honored Dewey on his seventieth birthday with a special tribute in the *Jewish Daily Forward* entitled, "John Dewey, America's Foremost Thinker," in which he wrote about Dewey for a Jewish audience in glowing terms:

> John Dewey is the most stimulating personality in the United States. . . . Spiritually he is the heir to Emerson and James. . . . Dewey's 70th birthday is an event which the whole intellectual world of America is celebrating. . . . Dewey is the prophet of intelligence as an adventure, his influence upon the life of the nation has been exercised at its source, upon the children through the teachers in the schools.[11]

At the same time that Kallen penned this first of many tributes to Dewey, the editor of the *Jewish Daily Forward* himself wrote a letter to Dewey on behalf of "our great *Forward* family throughout the country," offering congratulations on Dewey's seventieth birthday, and expressing his view of what Dewey symbolized for the Jewish immigrant masses: hope for Jewish survival in a new democratic America.[12] For Kallen, therefore, as well as for the Jewish immigrant masses, Dewey was certainly more than merely an eminent philosopher of American and international reknown; he was one of the key figureheads of the new era—imbued with modern, scientific, democratic, progressive spirit—which offered unparalleled freedom and opportunity for creative Jewish continuity.

Through their friendship and shared liberal political outlook, Kallen was able to enlist Dewey's aid from time to time in Jewish and general causes. In September 1936, Kallen organized eighteen other American professors, including Dewey, to refuse to attend a meeting of the German Philosophical Association in Berlin. This rebuff to the Nazis was given wide coverage in the American press. Kallen said that he and other philosophers considered the Berlin conference one in which "philosophy is but an apology for the ruling power."[13] Among the other signatories to the letter of protest were Irwin Edman, Alfred N. Whitehead, and Harry A. Overstreet.

In 1941, Kallen again enlisted Dewey's help in the Bertrand Russell Case. The case grew out of a churchman's assualt upon Bertrand Russell's person and principles after he was appointed to teach mathematics and philosophy in the College of the City of New York. Infuriated by this violation of academic freedom, Kallen convinced Dewey to write the introduction and an essay in a collection of essays that they coedited in a book entitled *The Bertrand Russell Case*.[14] Kallen himself wrote one of the major essays in the book, in which he lambasted what he called "the forces of antiquated religion" who fought against the forces of science and academic freedom. In listing some of the famous people who supported Bertrand Russell against the "fundamentalist clerics, machine politicians, and professional patriots" who sought to destroy him, Kallen included the name of John Dewey and called him "the foremost philosopher of America."[15]

Having collaborated together for over thirty years on different philosophical and political issues, it is no wonder that Kallen was one of the main organizers of Dewey's ninetieth birthday celebration in 1949, an event that was celebrated by the entire American and international intellectual community.[16] Kallen wrote this public tribute to Dewey:

> The word of John Dewey to the generations is summed up in the maxim that "all intelligent thinking means an increment of freedom in action, an emancipation from chance and fatality." Developed in his many works, this word has engendered a brave and responsible religion of human betterment wherever among men the mind is free and communication untrammelled. No philosopher alive or dead has so long retained the fullness of his powers. None alive has exercised so liberating an influence. His ninetieth birthday is a unique holiday for lovers of freedom everywhere.[17]

Although Kallen's first master was William James, his indebtedness to Dewey and his reverence for him as a philosopher-social activist was very deep.

In the late teens and early 1920s, Kallen was developing his own social philosophy vis-à-vis American society at the same time that he was enlarging his commitments to Jewish culture and the Jewish community, and these two concerns went hand in hand. He was the key link between Jewish and non-Jewish intellectuals, especially those who were concerned about one of the fundamental debates of American society at the time: whether America was to be conceived as a "melting pot" or as a culturally pluralistic society. In particular, it was his contact with Dewey that enabled the leading Jewish intellectual journal of the period, the *Menorah Journal*, to approach Dewey (through Kallen) to write an article for publication in its pages in 1917.[18] Dewey's article—the only one ever written by him to appear in a Jewish journal—bears a distinctively Kallenesque imprint in its strong support of cultural pluralism and Zionism. It was an important article for Jewish educators at the time (both Alexander M. Dushkin and Isaac B. Berkson referred to it in their dissertations), since it gave cultural distinctiveness (via Jewish education) a prestigious, intellectual basis in American society.

Dewey was concerned with the definition of nationality more in its cultural meaning than its political one. In describing the traits of nationality as community of language; community of literature; and a unity and continuity of tradition, history, and common memories, he emphasized the idea of cultural nationality.

> This community of tradition, ideas, and beliefs, or moral outlook upon the problems of life, which is perpetuated and more or less fixed by language and literature, creates a body of people somehow distinctly united by very strong ties and bonds. . . . It is certainly not the political unity or sovereignty which makes up such nationality but rather the cultural fact that people live together in community of intellectual life and moral emotion, of sentimental ideas and common practices, based upon common traditions and hopes.[19]

Dewey argued that while much attention had been paid to the rise of political nationalism in the nineteenth century, it was also important to note that that era had also been the time of an increasing rise in importance of all cultural nationality and national self-consciousness. Even though he differentiated between nationality in the cultural sense and nationalism in the political sense, he realized that in many cases the aspiration of cultural nationality to become an independent nation politically had been engendered by persecution, hostility, and lack of tolerance. He believed this to be the case for the Irish, the Poles, the Bohemians, and the Jews. In the interest of peace, Dewey argued for "a recognition of the cultural rights and privileges of each nationality—its right to its own language, its own literature, its own ideals, its moral and spiritual outlook on the world, its complete religious freedom—and such political autonomy as may be consistent with the maintenance of general social unity."[20] Political nationalism, as an outgrowth of cultural nationality, was considered legitimate as long as it abstained from war and promoted general social unity.

With regard to cultural diversity in the United States, Dewey believed that cultural give-and-take should be encouraged. He took a very strong stand against the melting pot theory of assimilation, supporting the idea of cultural pluralism (without taking it as far as Kallen did).

> The concept of uniformity and unanimity in culture is rather repellent. . . . Variety is the spice of life, and the richness and attractiveness of social institutions depend upon cultural diversity among separate units. In so far as people are all alike, there is no give and take among them. And it is better to give and take. . . . The theory of the melting pot always gave me rather a pang. To maintain that all the constituent elements, geographical, racial and cultural in the United States should be put in the same pot and turned into a uniform and unchanging product is distasteful. The same feeling that leads us to recognize each other's individuality, to respect individuality between person and person, also leads us to respect those elements of diversification in cultural traits which differentiate our national life. . . . Where there are many sorts of independent vigorous life, one provides nationality for interchange, for give and take of culture.[21]

Believing that a flexible and easy exchange between groups would stimulate the cultural creativeness of each group while simultaneously enriching the life of the nation as a whole, Dewey wanted America to be able to provide for each nationality an opportunity to cultivate its own distinctive individuality with only one limitation: it must not be allowed to become dangerous to the welfare of other peoples or groups.

Moving from cultural nationality to political nationalism, Dewey felt that political independence was generally impracticable for small nationalities. In the aftermath of World War I, it seemed clear that the principle of racial and cultural nationality could not be the basis for stable political organization for the future. Rather, while he supported provisions for cultural autonomy of nationalities, he strongly believed that provisions for economic interdependence were crucial for an enduring peace. Yet, he was willing to make an exception for Zionism, owing to the special circumstances of the Jewish people.

> At the present time it is extremely difficult to secure and maintain cultural freedom without some measure of definite political status. If I do not mistake, the cause of Zionism has great claims upon those who are interested in the future organization of the peaceful intercourse of nations because it not only guarantees freedom of cultural development in that particular spot in which the new nation is formed, but because it gives a leverage for procuring and developing cultural nationality in all the other countries which harbor within themselves large numbers of the Jewish folk. Moreover, the Zionist state would stand forth to the world as an inspiring symbol of victory against great odds, against seemingly insuperable odds, of the rights of nationality to be itself. From this point of view I feel that the Zionist movement is one that has a right to appeal to the

interest and sympathy of statesmen and of all who care for the future of the world's peaceful organization.[22]

This call for support of Zionism was based on its universalistic appeal as well as the particularistic situation of the Jewish people's inability to gain cultural freedom in most countries of the world. It is extremely likely that such strong support for Zionism, especially of "the right of nationality to be itself," on Dewey's part, derived from his contacts with Kallen during this period.[23]

Dewey had talked about the problem of nationality in education the previous year in an address to the National Education Association. He recognized the difficulty of developing the good aspects of nationalism without its evil side—of developing a nationalism that is the friend and not the foe of internationalism—but he did not abstain from facing the problem. Instead, he proposed that American education should cultivate two basic elements of its own nationalism. The first element was the fact that the American nation is itself a complex entity.

> Strictly speaking, it is inter-racial and international in its make-up. It is composed of a multitude of peoples speaking different tongues, inheriting diverse traditions, cherishing varying ideals of life. This fact is basic to our nationalism as distinct from that of other peoples. . . . Our unity cannot be a homogenous thing like that of the separate states of Europe from which our population is drawn; it must be a unity created by drawing out and composing into a harmonious whole the best, the msot characteristic, which each contributing race and people has to offer.[24]

Supporting the idea of unity with diversity, Dewey took a stand against separatism and favored hyphenism. He welcomed hyphenism "in the sense of extracting from its people its special good, so that it shall surrender into a common fund of wisdom and experience what it especially has to contribute."[25] In fact he argued that the genuine American is a hyphenated character; he is international and interracial in his make-up. Since the peculiarity of American nationalism is its internationalism, American education, in Dewey's view, needed to take more cognizance of this unique feature of American life.

Dewey's second basic point in the constitution of a genuine American nationalism was the need for equal opportunity for all. For him, to nationalize education meant to use the schools as a means for making this idea effective. This required changes in administrative methods that would put the resources of the whole nation at the disposition of the more backward and less fortunate groups.

> To nationalize American education is to use education to promote our national idea, which is the idea of democracy. This is the soul, the spirit, of

a nationalized education, and unless the administrative changes are executed so as to embody this soul, they will mean simply the development of red tape, a mechanical uniformity and a deadening supervision from above.[26]

If nationalizing American education meant essentially promoting a culturally pluralistic democratic society, then there was great hope for creative Jewish survival in such a society. This was the hope shared by Samson Benderly and the Bureau of Jewish Education group as well as Kallen and the Menorah Association group in the second decade of this century.

Though Dewey came out in support of cultural pluralism, his name was not as much associated with that idea as was the name of Horace Kallen. Kallen's articles in *The Nation* in 1915 had earned him a reputation as the arch-advocate of cultural pluralism.[27] Actually, Kallen's affinity for this idea—which became a lifelong cause as much as an idea—originated in the days when he served as assistant to George Santayana in a class at Harvard.[28] Given his philosophical training, it is no wonder that cultural pluralism implied more than a sociological meaning. For Kallen, it signified: "(1) a concept that social science and social philosophy can and do employ as a working hypothesis concerning human nature and human relations, and (2) an ethical idea—an article of faith which challenges certain prevailing philosophic conceptions about both those conceptions as fundamentally monistic."[29] In particular, the expression *cultural pluralism* was coined by Kallen to indicate a position with regard to individualism and community: "it postulates that individuality is indefeasible, that differences are primary and that consequently human beings have an indefeasible right to their differences and should not be penalized for their differences, however they may be constituted, whatever they may consist in—color, faith, sex, occupation, possessions or what have you."[30]

In his articles in *The Nation*, Kallen expressed the view that as the outcome of the European war, the United States was in the process of becoming a true federal state, a great republic consisting of a federation or commonwealth of nationalities. What was needed, he argued, was not a unison or uniformity, but a harmony of nationalities that would be concerned about the whole while granting a full measure of autonomy to the different groups in the orchestrated society. This was the way a democratic society like ours ought to function if it would be truly democratic. The various nationalities that compose the American commonwealth would have to learn that democracy means self-realization through self-control, self-government, and that one is impossible without the other. There were European analogies for this principle of harmony of nationalities within a society, of which Switzerland was the best example, according to Kallen, because it was a successful democracy that conserved and encouraged individuality. The reason for this, in his opinion, lay in the fact that in Switzerland the concept of "natural rights" operated, providing a psychophysical inheritance, whether consciously or unconsciously.

> Men may change their clothes, their politics, their wives, their religions, their philosophies, to a greater or lesser extent; they cannot change their grandfathers. Jews or Poles or Anglo-Saxons, in order to cease being Jews, Poles, or Anglo-Saxons, would have to cease to be. The selfhood which is inalienable in them, and for the realization of which they require "inalienable liberty," is ancestrally determined, and the happiness which they pursue has its form implied in ancestral endowment.[31]

By paying more attention to ancestral endowment and the inalienable rights of "national" groups, Kallen envisioned the outlines of a possible great and truly democratic commonwealth.

> Its form is that of the Federal republic; its substance a democracy of nationalities, cooperating voluntarily and autonomously in the enterprise of self-realization through the perfection of men according to their kind. The common language of the commonwealth, the language of its great political tradition, is English, but each nationality expresses its emotional and voluntary life in its own language, in its own inevitable aesthetic and intellectual forms. The common life of the commonwealth is politico-economic, and serves as the foundation and background for the realization of the distinctive individuality of each *nation* that composes it. Thus, "American civilization" may come to mean the perfection of the cooperative harmonies of "European civilization," the waste, the squalor, and the distress of Europe being eliminated—a multiplicity in a unity, an orchestration of mankind.[32]

In this conceptualization, the ethnic group assumes paramount importance. It is the "natural instrument" of the orchestra of society: its spirit and culture are its theme and melody, and the harmony and dissonances and discords of them all make the symphony of civilization, except that there is nothing fixed and inevitable about its progressions as in music.[33]

In the decade following the publication of his articles in *The Nation*, Kallen published several more essays dealing with the theme of American multiple group life, which were collected in a volume of his papers in 1924.[34] In these essays, and in subsequent writings throughout his career, Kallen emphasized three themes with respect to this theory of cultural pluralism. The first has to do with the nature of the ethnic group in its relation to the individual. Individuals generally affiliate with groups voluntarily, based on contractual relationships. The ethnic group, however, involves an involuntary affiliation, which depends upon ancestry and family connections. Thus, ethnic group membership and participation has special significance, which is of primary importance for personality growth and development. The second theme flows from his claim that his position is in harmony with the traditional ideals of American political and social life, much more so than any attempt at imposition of some Angle-Saxon sense of conformity. As he read it, American democracy ensured its citizens (and groups) the inalienable right to be different. The third theme, derived from the first two, asserts the positive value to the nation as a whole which has developed from the existence of various ethnic cultures and their interaction within the framework of a democratic society.[35]

All three of these themes were embraced by Jewish community leaders in the 1910s and 1920s, especially those most concerned with Jewish survival through Jewish education. The writings of Jewish educational leaders like Benderly, Berkson, Dushkin, and Emanuel Gamoran, reveal their strong sense of ethnic loyalty (largely through Zionism/Hebrew nationalism), their belief in the possibility of a synthesis between American and Jewish ideas and ideals, and their commitment to contribute their cultural share to America as they were enriched by American culture. Even if the specifics of Kallen's scheme of cultural pluralism were sharply criticized, Jewish educators upheld his general formulation, and attacked assimilationist trends.[36] Ascribing to the basic idea behind cultural pluralism, Jewish educators were indebted to Kallen, and they counted him among their ranks, even though he was not a practitioner (at least on the pre-adult level). Kallen remained involved in the higher levels of Jewish education as a vice-president of the American Association for Jewish Education, by his participation on numerous committees and commissions, and by espousing his ideas often in journals of Jewish education and culture.

Dewey's Influence on Kallen's Cultural Pluralism

Although Kallen acknowledged his general indebtedness and his great respect for Dewey, it is not clear how much this theory of cultural pluralism actually derives from Dewey's writings. In fact, this subject has been debated in educational literature. In a review of Seymour Itzkoff's *Cultural Pluralism in American Education*, it is argued that Dewey's theory of human nature does not provide a good philosophical basis for the ideal of cultural pluralism.[37] According to Itzkoff, Dewey implied that a culturally pluralistic society does not exist as an end in itself, but is the best social arrangement for leading to further changes. In Itzkoff's view, Dewey saw a pluralistic society as facilitating both a freer environment for personal individuality and the development of experimental intelligence. The value of pluralism for Dewey, however, was its furtherance of man's natural evolution, increasing his problem-solving abilities.[38]

Itzkoff claims that Dewey failed to recognize the uniqueness of culture.

In reality, there are no roots in Dewey's philosophy for a consideration of the real significance of differences in cultural outlooks. He is so interested in human thought and actions as instrumental to adaptive behavior that he has virtually omitted from his vision the significance of the uniqueness of culture. . . . Most crucial, Dewey did not come to grips with the fact that scientific logic, which he felt was the great hope for the democratic life, strives for unity for public truths, whereas cultures produce unique truths or values. This difficulty is heightened when we recall that Dewey polemicized constantly against the divisive sectarianism of religion as opposed to the social unification of science.[39]

Itzkoff regards Dewey's theory of human nature as inadequate, since he feels that it emphasizes one aspect of man's nature while ignoring or at least deemphasizing others. Yet, as Itzkoff himself admits, there are some roots in Dewey's philosophy for a doctrine of cultural pluralism, even if not in the details that Kallen might have liked. Kallen attempted to bring the spirit and even the letter of Dewey's philosophy to bear on the issue in which he was involved, namely, group survival vis-à-vis cultural pluralism; and he focused his analysis on the crucial element in Dewey's philosophy that equated the democratic society with the opportunities it provided for the fulfillment of individual capacities.[40]

It is no accident that those in the forefront of the development of the philosophy of cultural pluralism, like Kallen, were influenced by Dewey—at least to some extent—and were committed to his broad philosophical and educational goals. The pluralistic philosophy was seen as a supplement to Dewey's vision of a democratic dialogue of communities committed to the improvement of society.[41] For Kallen, however, the notion of cultural pluralism was viewed as integral to Dewey's and his own understanding of democracy.

While Dewey and Kallen shared some basic philosophical premises and held common positions on many important social issues, it is more than likely the case that Dewey was not the paramount influence on Kallen's development of his theory of cultural pluralism. There were other important influences: his study at Harvard, especially with William James and Barrett Wendell (to whom Kallen's most important work on pluralism, *Culture and Democracy in the United States*, is dedicated), his residence at the social settlement house in Boston's old North End during his college years (which led to his anti-assimilationist articles in *The Nation*), his reading of Theodore Parker and his conception of "The American Idea," and similarly his reading of James Truslow Adams's "American Dream" in his *Epic of America*. Steeped in the American literary and idealistic tradition, Kallen's level of indebtedness extended beyond that of Dewey and instrumentalism, to the broader American landscape, which included key individuals and events in his life.[42]

Despite appearances, Dewey was not the major source for Kallen's pluralism, and it has been argued that the fruits of his cultural pluralism diverged markedly from Dewey. The importance of the conception of identity, of the past, and of culture—which were the distinguishing characteristics of Kallen's social philosphy—were not shared by Dewey.[43] Specifically, Kallen and Dewey differed in their approach to individuality and individualism.

> Although Mr. Dewey and I are both pragmatists and own to the same general attitude toward the problems of life, of thought, and of the techniques by which these problems are to be attacked, there exists between us the inevitable differences which spring naturally from the differences of inheritance, background, training and experience. Chiefly, I think Mr. Dewey, in dealing with problems, is disposed to treat them in terms of "the Total situation" and to interpret items and parts as aspects mainly of "wholes" in which they figure. I, on the other hand, am disposed to start with the individual, and to interpret "wholes" as aggregations of and consequences from comparatively independent individual components.[44]

In contradistinction to Kallen, the starting point for reflection in Dewey is generally the social context within which all individuality was considered to exist. The individual could not be understood without relationship to the social context in which he finds himself. As opposed to seeing man in isolation, Dewey preferred to view man in association with other men—man growing more intelligent, becoming liberated—as he functions in some form of social environment.[45]

Kallen and Dewey differed not only on the question of individualism but also on their approach to community, especially about the individual's search for community. For Dewey, the search is mostly a problem-solving effort. He minimized the long-lasting, deep strength of ethnic ties: ". . . his grasp of culture is heavily laden with utilitarian purpose and strikingly devoid of deeper reasons for ethnic self-consciousness."[46] Also, for Dewey, community, not individuality, is the primary fact of existence. In contrast, Kallen's view of the search for community was quite dissimilar. Unlike Dewey, he acknowledged the importance and primacy of the early natural associations into which the individual is born. As noted earlier, he placed great importance in the "ancestral endowment" of ethnicity. Whereas Kallen's conception of ethnicity can be viewed as an extension of the eighteenth-century Enlightenment's doctrine of the natural rights of individuals extended to groups, Dewey refused to acknowledge "inalienable individual rights."[47]

Probably the main difference between Dewey's and Kallen's cultural pluralism revolves around the importance ascribed to ethnicity: "the two pluralisms depart not on the issue of individuality versus sociality, but on the fixity of ethnic allegiances in social evolution."[48] This emphasis on inherited ethnicity was carried to an extreme by Kallen, and even some of his Jewish comrades-in arms, like Berkson, felt that Kallen's assumptions about the existence of inherited racial-ethnic qualities violated democratic principles by predetermining the individual's fate. Moreover, Kallen's ideas about developing or strengthening ethnic enclaves in parts of America were too European and not adaptable to the American setting, which demanded adjustment to and integration within the new environment (even without "melting"). Kallen's ideas on this subject, however, were never turned into a practical blueprint for a truly intercultural society. Rather, they remained as pleas of poetical exhortation for the value of differences and the rights of the individual and the community. His call for cultural pluralism was his way of explaining—in evocative and even in metaphysical terms—his own deeply felt perceptions of the need to maintain cultural identity in the face of all the institutional and intellectual pressures of the modern world.

One more point concerning Dewey, Kallen, and cultural pluralism bears mention here. On the metaphysical-philosophical level, it must be noted that Kallen was much closer to his teacher, William James, than to Dewey with regard to pluralism. In an article, which was essentially a tribute to Dewey, he acknowledged his general indebtedness to Dewey but pointed out that he was philosophically closer to James's version of pragmatism (with its emphasis on plurality) than to Dewey's.

> The paramount value in James' philosophic faith was that Freedom for which the word in other contexts is chance, contingency, plurality, novelty, with Reason derivative, operational, a working tool. . . . The paramount value in Dewey's philosophic faith is Reason, whose right name is Intelligence and whose work is to liberate by unifying, organizing, controlling the kind of freedom to which James gives primacy. Dewey once called this path a nuisance, and stated that the task of intelligence is to emancipate the thinker alike from this nuisance and from fatality by working out a desired path through change and chance and necessity.[49]

Even with his affinity for James on this particular issue, Kallen shared the general tenets of pragmatism with both James and Dewey, and in fact regarded Dewey as somewhat of a successor to James, calling him "at once the greatest as well as the most venerable and most influential living prophet and teacher of this American faith."[50]

The Impact on Jewish Education

The doctrine of cultural pluralism advanced by Horace Kallen in the early decades of this century was accepted in principle by Jewish survivalists, especially Jewish educators, with their Zionist-nationalist leanings. Yet

Horace Kallen was not enough. They sought support for their right to preserve their unique cultural/national life among leading American intellectuals. They were looking for credibility and acceptability, and they found it in the writings and speeches of John Dewey, especially in his article in the *Menorah Journal* of October 1917 on "The Principle of Nationality," and in his address to the National Education Association, "On Nationalizing Education," in the previous year. In John Dewey, Jewish educators centered in the Bureau of Jewish Education in New York found "not only justification for educational change but [also] sanction for ethnic surival in democratic America."[51]

By associating him with the doctrine of cultural pluralism, Jewish educators were able to claim Dewey's support for the system of supplementary ethnic education that they were creating. Assuming cultural nationalism to be part of the free interplay of forces that were to shape America, then Jewish cultural nationalism was legitimate and should be an important educational force in American society. The fact that Dewey was wary of the potential evils of separatist tendencies was played down; what was important was that he had given the sanction for cultural pluralism and had spoken out vociferously against the melting-pot ideology that was anathema to Jewish educators.

Even if some of the leading Jewish educators of the time had read a little Dewey, they probably did not study his philosophy in great detail, and as a result they did not focus on the possible inherent dissonance between Dewey's social theory and methodology and their own. One must conclude that either they missed the point of some of Dewey's arguments—based on his adherence to scientific models of social and historical interpretation—or, perhaps, they simply chose to ignore difficult areas of disagreement that might not have meshed with their political purposes.

> The decision to utilize Dewey as a way to justify cultural pluralism and the supplementary religious school, might have had political significance. Perhaps Berkson, Kallen, Benderly and the others well understood the difficulties in Dewey's thought, and yet chose only to emphasize those elements in his philosophy that were advantageous to the political needs of the Jewish community, within an American society that was still pushing hard for the concept of the melting pot. Dewey's word carried authority, and leaving "nuances" aside, his thought was a powerful instrument for the justification of Jewish purposes within the society at large.[52]

Rather than going into detail in analyzing Dewey's thought relevant to its total relationship to the Jewish people and Jewish tradition, they hopped on the intellectual bandwagon of their times, subscribing to the religion of secular humanism, with its twin beliefs in the power of science and democracy to save. Kallen was probably the most devout secular humanist among Jewish intellectuals, yet he maintained that it was possible, even necessary, to

merge Judaism with secular humanism in what he called Hebraism or
Jewishness.

It may very well be the case that, in their desire to Americanize, Jewish
educators and community leaders relied too heavily on the secular humanism
of intellectuals like Kallen or Dewey, without realizing the potential threats to
Jewish authenticity and continuity in what they were doing. The spirit of
science, democracy, and humanism was very appealing and pervasive in
American intellectual thought at the time. Yet, would these systems of
thought and their concurrent methodology provide the necessary framework
and components for keeping the Jewish tradition alive and for passing it on to
the next generation? The record of the past half-century provides a negative
response to this troublesome question.

Notes

1. In the Jewish community, Kallen was a leader in the American Jewish Congress, YIVO, the Farband, the Labor Zionist Alliance, and the American Association
for Jewish Education, in which he served as vice-president for many years.

2. Kallen's Hebraism—his own unique secular-Jewish synthesis of Judaism and
modern culture—was best expressed in a book of essays published in 1932 entitled,
Judaism at Bay. In this book, subtitled "Essays Toward the Adjustment of Judaism to
Modernity," Kallen described what he meant by Hebraism, pp. 4–5: "It [Hebraism] is
the Jewish way of life become necessarily secular, humanist, scientific, conditioned on
the industrial economy, without having ceased to be livingly Jewish. Judaism will
have to be reintegrated with this secular, cultural form of community which is
Jewishness if Judaism is to survive." With his nonreligious yet cultural definition of
Jewishness, Kallen inevitably became an ardent Zionist, bringing to the American
Zionist movement American progressive values in an attempt to synthesize the best of
modern American and Jewish thought.

3. Sidney Ratner, ed., "Some Central Themes in Horace Kallen's Philosophy," in
Vision and Action: Essays in Honor of Horace M. Kallen on his 70th Birthday (New
Brunswick, N.J., 1953), p. 85.

4. See Ronald Kronish, "The Influence of John Dewey on Jewish Education in
America" (Ph.D. diss., Harvard Graduate School of Education, 1979).

5. Horace Kallen, interview by Kenneth W. Duckett, 20 May 1966; The John
Dewey Papers, Southern Illinois University, Carbondale, Ill., p. 3 (hereafter called
Dewey Papers, Illinois).

6. Ibid., p. 4.

7. Ibid., p. 5. Kallen related that during this period, Dewey would occasionally
join him and his friends at the movies, and they would all rise conspicuously when the
"Star-Spangled Banner" was being played (to demonstrate their patriotism, which was
suspect because of their left-liberal leanings!).

8. Letter from Horace M. Kallen to John Dewey, 14 October 1927; Dewey
Papers, Illinois.

9. Letter from John Dewey to Horace M. Kallen, 24 October 1927; Dewey
Papers, Illinois.

10. Horace Kallen, interview by Kenneth W. Duckett (see note 5 above), p. 6.

11. Horace M. Kallen, "John Dewey, America's Foremost Thinker," *The Jewish*

Daily Forward, October 1929; Dewey Papers, Illinois. This article was especially written in English by *The Forward,* which was a Yiddish newspaper of great importance to the Yiddish-speaking masses of New York Jewry at that time. At the same time, *The Forward* also published, in Yiddish, an editorial on 19 October 1929, in praise of Dewey on his seventieth birthday, and a three-page article on Dewey on 20 October 1929. In these two Yiddish pieces, much is made of Dewey's communal and societal concerns and activities and of his closeness to the goals of the labor movement although he was not officially a member of this group. (My thanks to Dr. Selma Parker of Northeastern University who read and reviewed these Yiddish articles for me.)

Kallen's tribute did not go unnoticed by Dewey. Upon receiving a copy of the article from the editor of *The Forward,* Dewey wrote to Kallen: "You treated me altogether too generously, but I was deeply touched by your kindness in writing it. It would be impossible to find a better expression of what I said, at least, would like to have said, no matter how far I have come short. Like a generous soul, you have penetrated behind the letter and said what I should like to have said if I had known how. I want not only to thank you, but tell you how much your friendship has always meant to me." (31 October 1929, Horace Kallen Papers [Kallen Papers], YIVO Archives, N.Y.).

12. Letter from B. C. Vladeck to John Dewey, 21 October 1929; Dewey Papers, Illinois. Vladeck wrote: "May you continue to be for millions of immigrants a symbol of a new America and a justification of their love for their new home." Vladeck also wrote to Dewey a year later to urge him to become head of the Socialist party in New York (letter from B. C. Vladeck to John Dewey, 10 July 1930, Dewey Papers, Illinois). Speaking for Jews who were politically involved in socialist-liberal circles, he appealed to Dewey to work with them in the political rejuvenation of the country. Clearly, some Jews certainly saw Jewish liberalism and American liberalism as coextensive, and looked to great social thinkers like Dewey, for guidance.

13. *New York City Post,* 16 September 1936, Kallen Papers, YIVO Archives, N.Y.

14. John Dewey and Horace M. Kallen, eds., *The Bertrand Russell Case* (New York, 1941). Actually Kallen had requested that Dewey be the sole editor for personal reasons, even though he was prepared to do most of the work. Kallen was worried about anti-Semitism: "The fact that I am a Jew is not precisely a help to the issue, and the fact that three Jews are contributing to this volume will, of course, be employed by the enemies in all sorts of ways to distract attention from the issue." (Letter from Horace M. Kallen to John Dewey, 4 April 1941, Kallen Papers, YIVO Archives, N.Y.). Considering the vociferousness of his attack, and the fact that this was in the midst of World War II, it is no wonder that Kallen anticipated anti-Semitic responses.

15. Horace M. Kallen, "Behind the Bertrand Russell Case," in *The Bertrand Russell Case,* p. 26.

16. Dewey even received a telegram from Chaim Weizmann, the president of Israel, which read: "On behalf of the people of Israel, I beg associate myself most cordially with tribute being paid today to America's great philosopher and preceptor. People of Israel take deep interest in Dewey anniversary celebrations not only because he was one of the earliest and staunchest supporters of Israel's cause, but also because his practical idealism and democratic activism conform significantly to their own spiritual tradition. May his great message help lead humanity back to reason and peaceful reconstruction." (19 October 1949; Dewey Papers, Illinois). Dewey's early, staunch support of Zionism will be discussed below.

17. 19 October 1949; Dewey Papers, Illinois. In addition to this public tribute, Kallen wrote a long personal letter to Dewey, expressing his gratitude for having had "a hand in the work and the fight (in the cause of human freedom and betterment) and to be able to count myself as one of your closer company" (20 October 1949). Kallen

also gave two public lectures that week, in honor of Dewey's ninetieth birthday: one at the New School for Social Research, entitled, "John Dewey, American," and one at Teacher's College, Columbia University, called "Human Rights and the Religion of John Dewey" (published in *Ethics* [April 1950]: 169–77).

18. Henry Hurwitz, the editor of *The Menorah Journal*, asked Kallen to send him Dewey's picture and autograph for publication (telegram, Henry Hurwitz to H. M. Kallen, 9 September 1917, Kallen Papers, American Jewish Archives, Cincinnatti). Hurwitz also sought Kallen's advice on speakers for the Menorah Society Convention of 1917, and Kallen suggested that the convention should face the problems of war in a spirit both of loyalty and of a liberal, democratic outlook, with intellectual leaders like Dewey to be invited. (Letter, Horace M. Kallen to Henry Hurwitz, 10 October 1917, Kallen Papers, American Jewish Archives, Cincinnati).

19. John Dewey, "The Principle of Nationality," *The Menorah Journal* 3, no. 4 (October 1917): 204.

20. Ibid., p. 205.

21. Ibid., pp. 205–6.

22. Ibid., pp. 207–8.

23. This was the time when Kallen was becoming increasingly active in the Zionist movement. For Kallen and other "messianic pragmatists" who were active in formulating American Zionist policy in the years 1914 to 1921, Zionism was designed to do two things: (1) to normalize the status of the Jews and thereby solve the "Jewish problem," and (2) to provide the means for the realization of an ideal state. See Sarah Schmidt, "Messianic Pragmatism: The Zionism of Horace M. Kallen," *Judaism* 25 (Spring 1976): 217.

24. John Dewey. "Nationalizing Education," *NEA Addresses and Proceedings*, 54 (New York, 1916); 184.

25. Ibid., p. 185. Kallen and Randolph Bourne had written important articles in support of the notion of the hyphenated American.

26. Ibid., p. 188.

27. Horace M. Kallen, "Democracy vs. the Melting Pot," *The Nation*, 18 and 25 February 1915.

28. Horace M. Kallen, "Alaine Locke and Cultural Pluralism" *Journal of Philosophy* 54(1957): 119.

29. Ibid.

30. Ibid., p. 120.

31. Horace M. Kallen, "Democracy vs. the Melting Pot," *The Nation*, 25 February 1915, p. 220.

32. Ibid.

33. Ibid.

34. Horace M. Kallen, *Culture and Democracy in the United States* (New York, 1924).

35. Milton M. Gordon, "Cultural Pluralism," chap. 6 in *Assimilation in American Life* (New York, 1964), pp. 144–47.

36. Ibid., p. 149. See especially Berkson's *Theories of Americanization* (1920), and Drachsler's *Democracy and Assimilation* (1920). Both Berkson and Drachsler postulated the desirability of promoting the preservation of the communal institutions of the ethnic groups and their cultures, but they also both argued for greater flexibility and alternatives of choice than was allegedly allowed by the Kallen presentation, and both were less optimistic about the long-term possibilities for the preservation of the ethnic groups and cultures under American conditions than was Kallen.

37. J. Theodore Klein, "Human Nature and the Ideal of Cultural Pluralism," *Educational Theory* 22, no. 4(Fall 1972): 479–84.

38. Ibid., p. 479.

39. Seymour W. Itzkoff. "Dewey and Cultural Pluralism," in *Cultural Pluralism and American Education* (Scranton, Pa., 1969), pp. 62–63. Itzkhoff points out there (p. 63), that Isaac Berkson's criticisms of Dewey were made on this point: "The emphasis Berkson placed on the stable discipline of traditional community values as a guard against the egoistic, individualistic tendencies in Dewey reflects his continuing concern with the implicit difficulties of the pluralistic aspects of Dewey's instrumentalism." It seems to me that Itzkoff slightly exaggerates his point here. To label Dewey as having "egoistic individualistic tendencies" is to ignore his great emphasis on social and community life. Also to say that he polemicized *constantly* against religion (while only citing one source, *A Common Faith*) is also a bit unfair.

40. Ibid., p. 54. both Kallen and Berkson quoted Dewey's famous speech in 1916 to the National Education Association, in which he stated that all Americans are hyphenated and that the American is international, interracial, and that our nationalism was a form of internationalism.

41. Ibid., pp. 46–47. Itzkoff adds: "Perhaps this quality of supplementation in Dewey's use of cultural pluralism explains the weakness in the movement as well as the insufficiently detailed proposals in Dewey's general writings on social philosophy."

42. Jay Wissot, "John Dewey, Horace Meyer Kallen, and Cultural Pluralism," *Educational Theory* 25(Spring 1975): 188. Wissot writes in opposition to what he felt was Itzkoff's overstatement of Deweyan influence on Kallen with respect to cultural pluralism.

43. Ibid., p. 195.

44. Kallen, as quoted in ibid., p. 190.

45. Wissot, ibid., p. 191. Wissot quoted from Dewey's *Democracy and Education*, *The Public and Its Problem*, and *Individualism: Old and New* to bolster his argument.

46. Ibid., p. 192.

47. Ibid., p. 193.

48. Seymour Itzkoff, "The Sources of Cultural Pluralism," *Educational Theory* 26(Spring 1976): 232. In this rejoinder to Wissot's article, Itzkoff reacts to Wissot's claim that he had exalted Dewey's impact on Kallen above all others. He argues that, on the contrary, he was trying to show that "the subsequent lack of impact on social and educational problems of the theme of cultural pluralism owed much to the failure of the leading social philosophy of that era (that of John Dewey) to account intellectually for pluralism." Further Itzkoff believes that "Kallen's explicit promulgation of cultural pluralism was fatally afflicted by its overall absorption into the intellectual milieu of Dewey and progressivism."

49. Horace M. Kallen, "John Dewey and the Spirit of Pragmatism," in *John Dewey: Philosopher of Science and Freedom*, ed. Sidney Hook (New York, 1950), p. 38. In fact, Kallen stated quite clearly with regard to this specific issue, "As for me, I stand here with James" (p. 39).

50. Ibid., p. 46.

51. Arthur A. Goren, *New York Jews and the Quest for Community* (New York, 1970), p. 119.

52. Eduardo Rauch, "Jewish Education in the United States" (Ph.D. diss., Harvard Graduate School of Education, 1978), p. 424.

On the Unity of the Kallen Perspective

ELMER N. LEAR

The content of this article has been gestating for some time. What brought it to full term was Spencer J. Maxcy's thought-provoking "Horace Kallen's Two Conceptions of Cultural Pluralism."[1] In this essay, Maxcy advances a two-Kallen thesis: Phase One, an early Kallen whose pluralism centered upon ethnicity, and Phase Two, a later Kallen whose pluralism relocated to the arena of vocation. Coordinated with each target area were to be found characteristic modalities for implementation: with ethnicity, "orchestration"; with vocation, "education." The presumed upshot of this analysis is that the student of American intellectual history, whether interested primarily in education or in sociocultural dynamics, must exercise due caution when invoking the concept of cultural pluralism—particularly when drawing upon Kallenian versions—lest he fail to disentangle the principal threads of application.

Immediately, this author must declare his repudiation of Maxcy's thesis. The contention is unacceptable because its documentary supports lean *primarily* upon Kallen's better-known sociopolitical and pedagogical writings, to the neglect of two essential literary species. These neglected classifications consist of Kallen's more technical philosophical output and his parochial (Jewish) treatises. The first category, generally acknowledged in prefatory lip service, is thereafter brushed aside without pertinent citation. The second is commonly ignored completely. This essay will draw upon these two groupings of Kalleniana in adopting the standpoint of the unitary rather than binary character of his cultural pluralism.

Before developing the main lines of argumentation, one should call attention to internal weaknesses in Maxcy's position, which serve to limit the force of his claims. First and foremost, nowhere does one find a line of demarcation separating the postulated two phases of Kallen's pluralistic outlook. Kallen enjoyed a long and fruitful life (1882–1974) and remained a prolific writer even during his closing years of infirmity. Maxcy supplies his readers with no watershed for differentiating between the two Kallens: neither sharp dates, nor change in institutional affiliations, nor shift in nonacademic involvement, nor other pertinent biographical data. The works cited by Maxcy overlap in publication dates, not falling neatly into early or later phases. In consequence, independent confirmation of the Maxcy thesis becomes extremely difficult.

Beyond this, Maxcy appears to hedge. *The Education of Free Men*, published in 1949, presumably falls into Phase Two, and interlocks with "vocation." Yet Maxcy acknowledges Kallen's prescription: "The schools are to recognize the vast ethnic diversity of American culture, to stress the contributions of these ethnic groups to life, and to teach respect for these differing nationalities, while cooperating with them."[2] Such recommendations would find apt application to the public education of Hispanics and Indo-Chinese in United States' schools of the 1980s and are most assuredly congruent with the alleged Phase One of Kallen's cultural pluralism.

With due respect to Maxcy's ingenious "revisionism," this author shall contend that Kallen's cultural pluralism remained unitary in conception. It is the merit of this doctrine that it is sufficiently flexible to be generative of multiple applications, not the least important being that of relevance for the field of "vocation." It will further be asserted here that Kallen's interest in the economic and occupational aspects of life had been integral with his ethnic concerns. Relatedly, with reference to implementation, it is straining at gnats to tease apart "orchestration" and "education" insofar as each is translatable and sometimes collapsible into the other.

By neglecting Kallen's "parochial" writings, Maxcy and others have done to Kallen what some interpreters have done to the thought of Martin Buber. These commentators have concentrated upon the universal motifs enunciated and have taken no notice of the particularistic themes. Both Kallen and Buber were drawn into a lifelong absorption with the culture and existence of the Jewish people in general and Palestine-Israel in particular. When addressing themselves to mankind at large, both men placed in the foreground global ecumenical tenets; when addressing themselves to a Jewish readership, they transferred to front-and-center more insular topics. Notwithstanding, the careful reader will find no incompatibilities in philosophy, only in scope and magnitude of issues examined. The explanation, in the case of Kallen, lies in a consistent adherence to an antimonistic metaphysic.

i

To understand Kallen is to appreciate the metaphysical foundation of his pluralistic outlook. Monism, for him, presents a false conception of the nature of reality. Consider his contrasting of the philosophies of Bergson and James, for illuminating commentary:

> . . . Bergson is before all things systematic, consistently architectonic, a monist who insists on an irrefragable difference between appearance and reality. . . . James, on the contrary, is before all things intent on insights and data rather than on system. His philosophy is a mosaic, not an architectonic. . . . For him there is everywhere a new beginning, and the piecemeal character of knowledge-of-aquaintance is rooted in the plural character of the reality that it apprehands. Thus, where Bergson beholds a universe, James sees a multiverse. . . .[3]

Kallen remained a lifelong disciple of James in dismissing a monistic metaphysic. As in the case of his master, he drew upon Darwinian thought to clarify his viewpoint:

> . . . If, then, we take the evolutionary hypothesis radically enough, we see a struggle for survival, a constant unification by adaptation, and a diversification by spontaneous variation, throughout the entire range of being. The universe, in a word, is tychistic.[4]

Ten years later, in his "Introduction" to the Modern Library selections from the corpus of James writings, Kallen offered his further appreciation:

> You do not need, says James, a One beyond experience to give birth to the Many of experience and hold them together in their own ways and of their own power.[5]

The objection is advanced; how can one make meaningful reference to the world while disregarding its unitary character? Kallen's response is simple:

> . . . Suppose you take the world at its face value. Suppose you don't look for a substance behind experience but accept your experiences for what they declare themselves to be when they arrive. . . . You find transition and change, continuity and discontinuity, routine and surprise, multiple unities of manifold kinds, . . . all connected with one another by transitions from next to next. . . .[6]

It does not follow that the pluralism he advocates is akin to self-contained, windowless monads, each of which constitutes a world unto itself. Kallen's pluralism is strongly influenced by Jamesian analysis expounded in *A Pluralistic Universe*. The key to understanding pluralism is found in taking "relations" seriously, in both a metaphysical and an epistemic sense: one must understand James's philosophy of pure experience

> . . . with its insistence on the experiential reality of relations, and on the metaphysical equality of all experiential entities. . . . Reality is a multi-

plicity, yet not that complete and utter externalization of qualityless points. . . . Now, if any one thing more than any other sets James beyond the philosophic tradition . . . , it is his readiness to take relations, conjunctive as well as disjunctive, internal no less than external, at their face value. . . . There is not a block of oneness that we call life, and a hegemony of bare homogeneous manyness that we call space, nor yet an ineffable *totum simul* which is, and still is *not* that, like Plotinos' One, rejecting both categories. There is a *real* combination of manyness and oneness in which the relations that bind, and whose action makes the oneness, are as immediate data of sense-perception as the terms that are bound; and the relations that distinguish, and whose actions make the manyness, have as legitimate a metaphysical status as the terms that differentiate. . . .[7]

As might be anticipated, Kallen's wide-ranging pluralism had its axiological ramifications. Over the decades, he seized upon many an opportunity to excoriate the classical tradition in philosophy, particularly Platonism, insofar as it embodied the "pathetic fallacy." On Kallen's allegation, traditional philosophy has hypostasized relations such as "good," "beautiful," "true," into substances, offering these desiderates as compensatory substitutes for the bitter disappointments of daily experience. Writing during World War I (but reaffirming his position by republishing the essay in a 1948 work), Kallen states:

In fact, experience as it comes from moment to moment is not one, harmonious and orderly, but multifold, discordant, and chaotic. Its stuff is not spirit, but stones, and railway wrecks, and volcanoes, and famine, and submarines, and trenches. . . . Plato . . . is the first explicitly to have reduplicated the world, to have set existences over against values, to have assigned absolute reality to the compensatory ideals. . . .[8]

Until the very end of his career, Kallen continued to ponder the relationship between existence and values. In a chapter of a meditative work dealing with the human predicament, he analyzes the grounds of his dissatisfaction with both "optimism" and "pessimism" as philosophies of life. *Meliorism*, a term introduced by James, comes closer to summing up Kallen's predilection:

. . . I believe that it orchestrates less discordantly than Optimism and Pessimism with the role of Creativity, Imagination and Logic in mankind's struggle to live on as Homo sapiens; . . . Recognizing the human predicament as a sort of Siamese twin of the human sapiency, Meliorism seeks not how to escape from it, but how to humanize it. In any Meliorist context value and existence are but two perspectives of an identical orchestration.[9]

The common version of monistic thinking, at least in the Western world, is found in the domain of religion, taking the form of a monotheistic theology. Subscribers to this creed, in its many varieties, organize themselves into religious communions. Kallen accuses them of degrading multiplicity and diversity, while seeking "proofs" to validate their elevation of Oneness. Metaphysically, they rely upon dialectical discourse. Their other mode is mysticism. Regarding the latter,

> . . . Its vehicle is some discipline of mind and body whose successive steps should consummate in a knowing of the Unknowable more certain and self-evident than the completest knowing of the Knowable. . . .[10]

For the mass of adherents to the popular Western religions, *their* conception of God is exclusively true and they tend to be intolerant of rival conceptions: "Their God is one as their country or king or Emperor is one—one by isolation from others, by denial of divinity to others. . . ."[11] His animadversion of antipluralistic religion is given bitter expression:

> On the record, religion is constituted by the self-conservation of each by force of its war upon all, by force of its always denying that others, however wrong it may believe them to be, have alike the same right to be wrong as it has to be right.[12]

Kallen spurns absolutist conceptions of religion and deity in favor of a Durkheimian approach:

> . . . If we regard religion as the "consciousness of the highest social values," God, who is the imaginative incarnation and concretion of these values, the one symbol of their manyness, becomes the social soul of which the institutions of society—economic, political, aesthetic and ritual—are the body. As psychologists know, for every change in the body there is a corresponding alteration of soul. The idea of divinity therefore has a history which may be considered as a function of the history of the society that entertains the idea.[13]

He deems himself a secularist, a conviction that he avers is consistent with the dictates of rationality, democracy, and pluralism:

> Secularism is a development of religion. It comes into existence when the ideal of equal liberty for all faiths and special privileges for none becomes a working hypothesis verifying itself in all the institutions of a culture. Then believers in creeds which are different from each other commit themselves to living with each other, not as feuding families but as good neighbors.[14]

Kallen's pluralism is applicable to many fields. Its relevance for linguistics is discussed in the course of a disquisition on the elusiveness of "precision":

> . . . the *élan* of human speech . . . keeps liquidating all would-be infallibilist fixations, keeps rendering their precisions imprecise, keeps suffusing anticipated meanings with unanticipated ones. Grammar and logic, rules

of usage and laws of thought work best like our traffic laws, effective when and as followed but with no power of their own over words and their ways in the flux of language. . . . Words like *symbol, metaphor, fable, allegory* and the like purport to signify sequences and compenetrations of meanings to which the precedents of usage and the laws of logic are either tangent, incidental, or irrelevant. Meanings just do not reveal themselves as the eternal and universal identities which our anxious quest of precision and certainty postulates.[15]

Aesthetically, monism was unacceptable to Kallen in that it stripped away life's charm and excitement, as it coated diversity with a monochromatic dullness. It is clear that an aesthetic interpretation of social life contributes significantly to supplying Kallen's insights and metaphors. It is this dimension that he utilizes in demonstrating the relationship of diversity and consensus:

Often an ancient maxim is called up to check the warfare of authority against freedom. The maxim is *De gustibus non est disputandum*, which has stood as an aphorism in the proverbial wisdom of the Western World's latinity. . . . The record falsifies the dialectic of both monistic esthetic absolutism and monadistic esthetic pluralism. It was not incommunicability that the anonymous aphorist had in mind when he pronounced his *De gustibus*. It was liberty he had in mind, and liberty as being the ground and condition of communication. It is when taste is free, when man is in cultural fact as in natural disposition the measure of beauty as of truth and goodness, that communication flows and dispute flourishes. Far from being beyond dispute, no field of interest is so fertile of dispute as taste. . . .[16]

Writing during World War II, when the Soviet Union was an ally of the United States, Kallen hoped there might be a relaxation of restrictions upon Soviet artistic expression:

Perhaps, because of our alliance, the government and people of Russia may themselves move to restore to the Russian artist and thinker the liberty without which no science and no art can live or grow. Perhaps the government and people of Communist Russia will refuse to endure that the artists of their land should have exercised a liberty under the Czars which is denied them under the Commissars. The religion of Freedom which is the art of *live and let live*, grows by what it feeds on, and it feeds on itself; the more of it men have in their works and ways, the more they need, the more they get and the more they want.[17]

The high valuation Kallen always applied to cultural creativity had its wellspring in his aesthetic sensitivity, and not alone in his political and sociological interests. The creativity he sought for, whether among the component ethnic enclaves of a pluralistic nation like the United States, in Palestine/Israel, or among the small independent nation states of a world society, led him to sage and penetrating observations in the course of world travels. What but the practiced eye of an accomplished aesthetician would elicit the rather caustic commentary on the scene in Warsaw, Poland, in the late 1920s?

> . . . this culture is like the product of all the neo-nationalist endeavors to manufacture a culture as one manufactures a shirt—linguistic chiefly; consisting in resaying in Polish what has been better said in other media. It copies the fashions in Europe instead of uttering the style of life in Poland. And in this respect the new Poland is no better than the old. Her endeavor after a Polish national culture is intensified. It seems to consist of two activities. The more passionate and vigorous one, as is the historic wont of the Poles, is to repress and shut out what is different but is so near as to be a possible rival. The other is to copy without assimilating, to lay on, but not absorb the alien beauties into the stream of feeling and action which nourished the national life. Both processes are called polonization. The first converts the helpful neighbor into a perilous one. The second petrifies and arrests what should melt down and flow freely. . . . The perfect example of both these processes in polonization you may behold on the great Saxon Square of Warsaw.[18]

In Kallen's search for metaphor to express his pluralistic orientation, his selection of the term "orchestration" was most apt. The inexactitude of the term may provoke consternation in some readers (such as Maxcy). Yet, it would be difficult to find a substitute better suited to convey an individuality blending into a larger whole, but permitting disengagement and retrieval of this individuality. Apparently Bertrand Russell had come upon the same expression when commending a form of human association that encouraged diversity, freedom, and creativity. Kallen cites Russell with approval, as the latter set forth his ideas in *New Hopes for a Changing World* (p. 181):

> . . . A great society for us is one which is composed of individuals, who, so far as is humanly possible, are happy, free and creative. We do not think that individuals should be alike; we conceive society as like an orchestra, in which the different performers have different parts to play and different instruments upon which to perform, and in which cooperation results from a conscious common purpose. . . .[19]

In point of fact, the distinguished colleague of William James, Harvard philosopher Josiah Royce, had occasion to employ Kallen's favorite term in his 1913 work, *The Problem of Christianity:*

> But the true community . . . depends for its genuine common life upon such cooperative activities that the individuals who participate in these common activities understand enough to be able, first, to direct their own deeds of cooperation; secondly, to observe the deeds of their individual fellow workers, and thirdly to know that, without just this combination, this order, this interaction of co-working selves, just this deed could not be

accomplished by the community. So, for instance, a chorus or an orchestra carries on its cooperative activities. In these cases cooperation is a conscious art.[20]

Is it indispensable that a directing personality or force, a maestro, presiding over the grand harmonies be identified? No, not from Kallen's viewpoint:

> Every local or national culture has an international cultivation. Their ways and works compose a federal union, not a centralized unity. This union is a self-patterning process, wherein an ever-changing One takes form as the orchestration of an ever-changing Many. . . .[21]

ii

Having located the bedrock upon which Kallen grounded his rejection of monism, one may now refer to his espousal of the derivative and widely known *cultural pluralism*. It is well to remember that the social realities perceived by this thinker always remained part of the philosophic domain. Let a philosopher uphold an antimonistic metaphysical position and he tends to opt for an antiauthoritarian sociocultural world.

Kallen always insisted that the ultimate unit of a society is the individual, and it is his well-being that constitutes the most reliable measuring rod of a community's virtue and success. The individual within a social complex is not the less an individual because of his civic responsibilities:

> Thus, the current conventions of science and industry impose a subordination of the Many to the One, a regimentation of work, play, and learning. . . . Every man knows in his heart that however much he may be coerced, his individuality always overflows every formula, falsifies every measure, nullifies every scale and finally escapes every coercion.[22]

Kallen looked out at the world of the 1920s and 1930s and saw the horrible consequences of the thrust toward sameness:

> The men and women of Japan, of Italy, of Russia, of Germany (particularly of Germany where it has assumed the ardors and grotesqueries of a mass-paranoia), all manifest the workings of the same craving. . . . But, whatever its architecture, it provides the figure of a victorious One, reconciling, subordinating, harmonizing the centrifugal Many. The equivalents to Plato's Republic generated by these times are prevailingly Communism and Facism. . . .[23]

Expressing himself in prose, Kallen intones an ode to the free society:

> The free society: The free society is a society of hazard, of insecurity, struggling to maintain and enlarge the union of the diverse which it

constitutes by enabling unlike and like freely to come and go, yet hold together amid a circumambience of configurations— . . . alike among the infinitely small and the infinitely great, in sequences of unions, separations, fights, flights, and reunions. . . .[24]

Kallen elaborates, invoking America's basic instruments of government as the buttress rendering secure the coveted individual rights:

The propositions of the Declaration of Independence are the postulates upon which all the later affirmations rest. . . . It is necessary to remember that, when the Declaration was made, the world was everywhere caste-dominated and class-ruled; . . . that the ideal and the law were conformity and submission to the ruling powers in faith, in morals, in politics, in study, in occupation, and in all similar matters. . . . The American way of life, then, may be said to flow from each man's unalienable right to be different, as this is enchanneled in the American Constitution. . . .[25]

It is clear that Kallen is almost without peer in his stalwart defense of the individual's indefeasible right to self-development and self-expression. Nevertheless Maxcy is in error, isolated quotations to the contrary notwithstanding, when he asserts that Kallen split with John Dewey over the latter's linkage of the individual "with the social in order to define him."[26] Why then did Kallen attack European liberalism, if not over this issue? With strong endorsement, Kallen invokes the views of the jurist Louis D. Brandeis:

The failure of liberalism is coincident with the oppression of nationality: "enlightened countries grant to the individual equality before the law; but they fail to recognize the equality of whole peoples or nationalities. We seek to protect as individuals those constituting a minority, but we fail to realize that protection cannot be complete unless group equality also is recognized."[27]

Kallen's underscoring of the rights and freedoms of the individual, in keeping with his philosophic views, is inseparable from his preoccupation with the status and interrelationship of groups. After all, individuals do not live a life of isolation, and the dynamics of intergroup existence impinge upon individual prosperings and sufferings:

Yet it seems to me that the record, as psychologists and historians view it, takes account of liberty chiefly in terms of groupings; that it does not deny the actuality of groups—at least not of the States and certainly not of the races, sects and cults within them. . . . The American Union begins, on the record, as a Union of Unions, and of Unions with Unions, each with its own specific, concrete medium, method, and aim of association. Of course, the elemental term in every such union is, as I have always urged, the individual in his indefeasible singularity.[28]

These groups enjoy an existence, at one level of analysis, distinct from that of the individuals composing them. There is nothing supernatural or mystical about these group identities. They constitute the subject matter of investigation and analysis on the part of cultural anthropologists and sociologists:

> The group culture will seem to have a nature independent of them all [the individuals]; to be a whole different from its parts, with ways and works evincing its own different laws of persistence, struggle and growth, and capable of determination without reference to the dynamic specificity of the parts. . . . If the individuals of the culture are psychosomatic organisms, the culture is a super-organic psychosoma. . . . It is their overruling providence, the shaper of their fates and fortunes, with a cyclical life history peculiar to itself. . . .[29]

In a normative sense, what is the relationship of groups toward one another? Kallen explicates his pluralistic approach by drawing upon the sciences:

> Sciences postulate the oneness of the many in two modes. One is exemplified by a repetition of identicals such that, at long last, repetition is condensed in a continuing sameness . . . in every scientific "law." The other is exemplified by a whole or totality whose parts are so related to one another that none can exist or alter independently of the others. . . .[30]

The ideals of the United States, though tarnished by "intermittent segregative and isolationist diversions," correspond to that brand of pluralism associated with Kallen's social philosophy. These ideals stand in opposition to a notion of the Americanization process metaphorically termed the *melting pot*. Kallen cites with approval the words of Harold B. Hoskins:

> . . . our American ideal should be expressed not in terms of a "melting pot" with its somewhat mournful implication of uniformity, but rather in terms of an orchestra, in which each racial group, like an orchestral choir, contributes its special, different tone to the rich ensemble of the whole.[31]

To speak of majority and minority populations is philosophically wrongheaded:

> . . . "majority" and "minority" mean to free men associative and functional relationships of groups and individuals, not constitutive organs of unchanging societies. When you take together *all* the people who are we the people as one Association, any and every lesser combination of the people, no matter how large, is a minority, and *we the people* is but the orchestration of minorities into the singularity of the national being.[32]

The culture of the United States of America is in reality intercultural, and is joined with the concepts, interfaith and interracial:

> All three denote conscious ends and conscious means to attain the ends. All three are descriptive of the goals and methods in a teamplay of churches and of governments, urban, state and federal, as well as of voluntary *ad hoc*

societies. The intent is in the common prefix: *inter,* which here postulates the parity of the different and their free and friendly communication with one another as both co-operators and competitors; it postulates that every individual, every society, thus realizes its own being more freely and abundantly than it can by segregation and isolation and struggle to go it alone.[33]

iii

It is extremely difficult, if at all possible, to separate Kallen's devotion to the American creed from his preoccupation with Jewish survival and his laudation of the Hebraic spirit. One can readily make a case for the concomitant applicability of his cultural pluralism to American life, the comity of nations, the internal democracy of the American Jewish community, and the viability of a sovereign Jewish state in the world. In a world liberated from intolerance and dictatorships, it is elementary to assert that anti-Semitism and the endemic threat to Jewish physical existence would be no more. The possibility for Jewish creativity, however, requires something more. It is appropriate then that one take up Kallen's notion of what it means to be a Jew. The notion of Jewishness has been much debated and has lent itself to considerable theorizing. Kallen explains:

> It is profoundly true that to the outer world a Jew is a Jew, a fact, one and indivisible. The situation is not, however, so simple. The fact Jew, is not defined alone by the attitude of the Gentile. It is defined also by the character of the Jew, his historic character, his social character, his spiritual character.[34]

Kallen abhors the reductionist proposition that defines Judaism exclusively as a confessional faith:

> You cannot convert the Jewish community into a mere sect without destroying Judaism. Judaism as Judaism can flourish only in the organic wholesomeness of Jewish communal life, with its checks and counterchecks, its conflicts, adjustments, and balancings of opposed parts. Only by reintegrating Judaism into wholeness can it be saved. . . . You cannot separate any social institution from the natural community-complex of which it is a part.[35]

In resounding terms, Kallen called upon his fellow Jews to recognize their group identity. This view ties in with his epistemological position that relations are to be taken seriously:

> No individual can be emancipated through, in, and for himself. He can only be emancipated for himself in and through his group. First and foremost, he must have freedom of association with the members of his group; he must have the right to express himself through the common life

of his group. The word "Jew" is a collective term, not an individual term. It designates an associative relationship.[36]

The general secularistic stand adopted by Kallen transferred over to his definition of Jewish existence:

> In history the culture of the Jews appears as no mere religion; in the world's count of it, it receives another name and a different estimate. It is called Hebraism, not Judaism, and to be a lover of Hebraism is more than to be a Judaist. . . . Hebraism, what "Israel has stood for in history," is the life of the Jews, their unique achievement—not as isolated individuals, but as a well-defined ethnic group. . . .[37]

Inferences drawn from the past are applicable to the present:

> Problems of civic status, economic security, cultural improvement make it necessary for the Jews of the world, as for other groups, to come together to consult about their Jewish problems, . . . to reach a consensus concerning principles and policy. Even if we wanted to be separated from one another, the conditions of modern life would not let us. For this reason, Jewish unity must embrace in the form of proper organization all the Jewish communities of the world.[38]

Some interpreters of Kallen have read into his cultural pluralism notions alien to his most profound convictions. For one, Spencer Maxcy, in differentiating between "two Kallens," asserts that the early Kallen "supported the idea that national origins predetermined an individual's creative abilities," whereas the later Kallen "de-emphasized the notion of inherited ethnic abilities."[39] The crucial term in this allegation is *abilities*. Kallen does not impute (and subsequently withdraw the imputation of) inborn *abilities* to individuals of any nationality. Rather, his position comes closest to that of such an anthropologist as Ruth Benedict whose "patterns of culture" supplied the raw materials drawn upon by individuals reared in a given society. Kallen's contention was that individuals, no matter how "creative," if reared in a colorless cultural conglomerate, a melting pot if you please, are working with synthetic materials, and, as traditionless cosmopolitans, lack verve. This insight had been grasped by the "Russophiles" of czarist Russia, in urging abandonment of French and Prussian influences in favor of a return to authentic peasant sources. The same insight has found repeated expression among American blacks in the "Harlem Renaissance," in Alex Haley's *Roots*, and elsewhere. It is a far cry from racist theories!

iv

To the observer of the American Jewish scene, there unfolds before him a variegated tapestry of national origins, denominational affiliations, organizational involvement, life styles, and attitudes toward the political economy of the United States. The pluralism that holds true today was even more accentuated during the decades prior to World War II, when one encountered a thriving American Jewish proletariat (including impressive activity in the labor movement and various shadings of socialist causes) and an animated Yiddish culture. The profusion of organizations and value choices provided Kallen with an abundance of raw material for testing his doctrines of democracy and freedom, his commitment to the voluntary orchestration of diversity, and his unquenchable faith in the potency of acquiring education.

One of the great challenges to the American Jewish community occurred during World War I, when both the rank and file and the leadership were preoccupied with the peace process. What type of deputation would voice Jewish interests at the peace conference, how representative of the broad sweep of Jewish alignments would this deputation be, how would they battle for a minorities clause in the peace treaty to prevent the future carnage of East European Jews and other hapless refugees, how would they promote the cause of a Palestinian Jewish National Home? These and other vexing questions furnished an acid test for Kallen's democratic pluralistic theory, both in the United States and overseas. Also Kallen himself became embroiled in many facets of the peacemaking and rehabilitational processes.

An important concatenation of socioeconomic forces within the United States Jewish community supplied the catalyst for the blending of Kallen's democratic and Jewish survivalist commitments. At the time of World War I, the American Jewish community consisted *primarily* of two elements: a small, upper class of German or Iberian provenance, Reform in synagogue affiliation and dominating communal agencies; the other, impoverished or lower middle-class masses, mostly of East European background, either religiously Orthodox or secularly socialistic. Both segments were horrified over reports of atrocities committed against their coreligionists in Eastern and Central Europe, and pleaded for international intervention. The dominant element sought to concentrate protest activities in its own hands, and was frigid toward Zionist "solutions." Its instrument par excellence was the American Jewish Committee, led by wealthy, conservative notables. The rank and file demanded a representative assembly, and tended to be ardently pro-Zionist. Kallen's democratic pluralistic inclinations placed him in the camp of those calling for an assembly representing *all* sections of American Jewish life, with strong backing for Zionist approaches. He set forth his ideas emphatically:

> The impact of American institutions and conditions showed itself in new arrangements and groupings of the Jews, in a new intellectual and social vigour which is attested by the periodical literature of the interval. . . . So far as the internal affairs of the Jewish community were concerned, it showed itself in a growing resentment against the tutelage of the traditional *Sh'tadlanic* [self-appointed, aristocratic] leadership. . . . The community

cried for something which should be done collectively. . . . This blind feeling and inarticulate cry crystalized into a philosophy of group solidarity and group-responsibility in the conception of a democratically constituted congress of American Jews. . . . It was a notion that precisely for this reason unsettled the old leaders and filled them with uneasiness and resentment. . . . There was established a Congress Organization Committee, of which Mr. Justice Brandeis was made the honorary head. . . . When it seemed that popular sentiment was overwhelmingly in favour of the Congress movement, the American Jewish Committee conceded the democratic plans, and that constitutes the fundamental victory for modernism in Jewish communal life in America.[40]

Shortly before the United States plunged into the herculean effort of the Second World War, a time when extremist right wing movements were still above surface, Kallen was preoccupied with the agonies of Jewish existence in Europe and the mission of Jewish agencies at home. In a notable article Kallen explored the role of the American Jewish community centers. Again he exhibits his devotion to the ideals of democratic freedom within a framework of cultural pluralism, demonstrating his unique blend of synoptic vision and particularistic affirmative action:

Jewish interest as a whole . . . should regularly be planned in such a way as to exhibit and clarify its dynamic link and interplay with other non-Jewish interests. . . . Every culture is at once a product of and a contribution to the Cultural Pluralism which constitutes the spirit of civilized mankind. . . . All cultures are most easily and directly communicated and most readily understood and appreciated through their arts. The Center should make the most of this fact. An essential of its program could be so to perfect positive, distinctly Jewish expression in the arts—in painting and sculpture, in music, drama, the dance—that the non-Jewish fellow members of the greater community will spontaneously look upon such expression as an asset and wish on their own account to preserve and strengthen it.

And, of course, the Center should cooperate with non-Jewish groups on specific issues involving the general principle of democracy—issues of civil liberties, for example, of civic rights and obligations. Since Jews are especially dependent for their status and right on democracy, they have a special obligation in defense of democracy. . . .

We cannot both be in flight from Judaism and fight effectively as Jews for democracy. We cannot accept the benefits of democracy outside the Jewish community and reject its obligations inside the Jewish community.[41]

Kallen's pluralism never passively contemplated fracturing and disintegration, whether he was engaged in surveying the larger American scene or the delimited American Jewish community. On the occasion of the (1954) Tercentenary celebration of Jewish settlement in these United States, he remarked forcefully:

. . . On the face of it, the centrifugal trends in American Jewry remain preponderant. . . . But that they will continue so is a conclusion disregarding the ongoing democratization of all sorts of Jewish groupings. On every level, each is different from the others; on every level they pool their differences in a communion, not in order to suppress or abolish them, but in order to assure to them equally the liberty, the safety, the support and strength they could not acquire by isolating themselves. They follow the American way, which is the way of liberty and union, on all levels of association. . . . Thus, with the celebration . . . the most vital, most prosperous and strongest Jewry in the world today is clarifying the choice between social self-preservation and social suicide as a community of free men.[42]

With becoming pride, a pride devoid of boastful chauvinism, Kallen etches out the mutuality of enrichment afforded by the enveloping American and embraced Jewish communities:

This community is established in and through the Old Testament, which contributes so largely to the singularity of the Jewish psyche: Lecky wrote that "the Hebraic mortar cemented the foundations of American democracy." But furthermore, the Jewish community, like every other composing the national being, serves as a psychological locale for voluntary social experimentation, for invention and discovery, as such, involving more limited risks than a nation-wide adventure would. Thus the Jewish locale has been an area of trial and error in employer-employee relations, in philanthropy, in education, in literature and in the arts. What was started in the Yiddish theaters of the East Side more than once was perfected—or corrupted—on Broadway; what began as a protocol on relations between Jewish employers and Jewish employees in women's wear has become the initiating precedent in the national growth toward industrial democracy; what began as an effort to help immigrant "coreligionists" cheaply and efficiently, has contributed to the formation of the theory and practice of scientific charity, and so on. And it is not possible to call these developments more an Americanization of Jewry—even of the Jewry of Palestine—than an enrichment of the American way by Jewish contributions. "American Jewish living" makes an impression of a healthy symbiosis with the diverse other forms of living whose interaction orchestrates the Union we call America, and whose combined utterance is the American spirit.[43]

v

At this juncture, it is essential to affirm that the proper locus of Kallen's cultural pluralism is not the United States but the global arena. Throughout his life, Kallen clung to the position that all *peoples*, not individuals alone, incarnate a basic urge toward creative self-expression. When permitted free scope, this urge not only imparts a vitality and vibrancy to collective existence but enriches the cultural resources of the entire world. This doctrine, universal in its applicability, found specific embodiment in his sentiments toward his own ethnic group. He strongly supported the creation and nurturing of a soverign Jewish state in the Land of Israel.

There are no cryptoracist undertones in Kallen's Zionism. He grounds his Zionism upon the realities of ethnicity and collective historic experience. The substantive content of this experience he terms Hebraism. If Hebraism is to be a vital force in today's world, it requires a geopolitical base:

> Historically, the basis of culture has always been ethnic and geographically political. . . . That the Jews, in classic times, have had these properties I need not argue. That they now have racial unity is properly enough disputed; that they have nationality the "diaspora" would seem to preclude. As the only evidence and guarantee for the future efficacy of the Jews as a group must be their past, their history. . . .[44]

Kallen's contribution to the development of Zionist thought is duly noted by an astute antagonist, the Egyptian political scientist, Abdelwahab Elmessiri. He adverts to a mystical strain in Kallen's Jewish nationalism:

> Even a supposedly level-headed pragmatist such as Horace Meyer Kallen, the American Zionist educational thinker, accepts this mystical view of Israel. He believes that the memories, hopes, and fears, the creeds and codes, and the works and ways of Israelis invest their national struggles with sacredness. The mysticism transvalues "the brute stuffs" of their daily lives. . . . The sanctity or divinity of the Jewish people, or its "naturalistic supernaturalism," if we may borrow one of Kallen's terms, is the common ground on which nonreligious and religious Zionists meet.[45]

A sense of history combined with a demand for justice impels Kallen to proclaim:

> We do not need Palestine because we are in exile. Being at home and not in exile, we still need Palestine . . . because its existence, its growth and freedom would right an ancient wrong; because they would achieve for all Jews—that equalization of status for their group which all nationalities claim and struggle for and must achieve.[46]

Jews call upon the world for benevolent assent:

> What do the Jews ask? . . . Only that . . . they may at long last live their lives in freedom and earn their bread in peace wherever they may be among the peoples of the earth, or in the Homeland of the Jews, the Homeland which they have earned a hundredfold, with their blood and treasure and sweat and tears. . . .[47]

With Zionism as the instrument for resurrecting a Jewish nation-state, Kallen was convinced the world as a whole would gain:

. . . Zionism is the solution of the Jewish problem because, if the past is any warrant for the future, there is every reason to believe that with the Jews as a free people in Palestine or elsewhere, that unique note which is designated in Hebraism has a chance to assume a more sustained, a clearer and truer tone in the concert of human cultures, and may genuinely enrich the harmony of civilization.[48]

Neither in the United States nor elsewhere in the world were Jews of one mind in endorsing a Palestinian Jewish Homeland. In this country, at the time of World War I, the Zionist question accelerated the democratic internal organization of American Jewry:

One consequence of the controversy over Zionism which ran from high to low through the communities was to bring to the fore the issue of community organization and community control. . . . American Israel divided . . . into two camps. The elder is represented by the American Jewish Committee, whose tradition is to think of the community as a somewhat hierarchical body governed by its elders—elders by virtue of birth, wealth, power, station, and superior education. . . . The younger and later is represented by the confederation of Jewish societies of all sorts and conditions called the American Jewish Congress, whose aspiration is to reach decision on the policies and programs of the community via the democratic process. . . .[49]

Indeed, the issue became a leaven, quickening the tempo of both intellectual and political expression:

The controversy over Zionism became a major force in the process of Americanization. It stimulated community organization, theological reorientation, historical and social research, and literary expression. It enriched the educational enterprises with new drives, new themes, new methods, new men, new standards. It brought both Hebrew and Yiddish into the dynamic foreground of expression, and it redirected the thinking about Jewish relations among Jews and non-Jews alike. It also has come to a consensus in which . . . ideological conflicts remain entirely compatible with united co-operative effort on behalf of Jewish Palestine.[50]

Understandably, there are those who ask with incredulity or with malice, "If Kallen takes cultural pluralism as a cardinal principle, how [do you] explain a devotion to Zionism with its Jewish cultural preoccupations?" Are the Arab Palestinians and their culture being supplanted by force majeure? Kallen's vindication of the Zionist enterprise, reiterated in many contexts, takes this characteristic form:

. . . the Koran, as well as Western religion and culture, peculiarly identifies Israel with Palestine and Palestine with Israel. Not since the days of the Judges has there been a Palestine without Jews. Whoever may have been the ruling power in Palestine, Jews were always both native in Palestine, and migrating to Palestine. After the Balfour Declaration, which gave the force of international law to this religious, social and cultural bond between the people the land, Jews began to immigrate into Palestine in greater numbers.

The land they bought to settle on was for the most part wasteland. The people among whom they settled was a stationary population, for the most part an illiterate, disease-ridden, pauper neolithic folk in bondage to feuding tribal leaders of wealth and power, such as the Husainis and Nashashibis. . . . The Jews own nothing in Palestine they have not paid for many times over. Their labor with that land caused a desert to bloom. It set going a democratic society on principles of free association in cooperative effort—the only center of democracy as a way of life anywhere in the Near East. It raised the standard of living of the Palestinian fellah. It increased literacy. It improved social and personal hygiene and reduced infant mortality.[51]

Between the Arab masses and the Jews of Palestine, Kallen could find no conflict of basic interests:

For fundamentally, the cause of the Jewish Homeland and the cause of the Arab fellah are one cause. I do not think that Zionist spokesmen have made this fact sufficiently clear to the enlightened opinion of the world. What the Amir Feisal, spokesman for the Arabic-speaking peoples, declared in 1918, and repeated many times thereafter, remains true in principle. . . . We are working for a revived and reformed Near East, and our two movements complement one another. The Jewish movement is national and not imperialist. . . .[52]

The global struggle of World War II definitely cast the Arab leadership on the side of the Axis powers:

On the record, the masters of the Arabic-speaking peoples have from the beginning aligned themselves in faith and in deed with the enemies of democracy. On the record, they oppose the Jewish Homeland because that is a center of democratic influence making for higher wages and a higher standard of living for the fellah whom his masters wish to continue to exploit as it pleases them. On the record, what is called Arab nationalism is a cynical Arab fascism exploiting the poverty, the ignorance and the religious fanaticism of the enslaved multitudes of the Arabic-speaking peoples of the Near East. . . . Arabic-speaking rulers are now making public announcements of their claims and demands, calling conferences to formulate their proposals . . . which threaten destruction and death to the Jewish Homeland. . . . In the United States, agents of Near Eastern Arab wealth and power and American oil interests have launched a propaganda of lies about Arab democracy, and rumors have been thick that certain officials of the State Department were not unsympathetic.[53]

Ten years after the establishment of Israel as a sovereign Jewish state, Horace Kallen made a study-trip to that land and offered this assessment:

The total impression I left Israel with was of a somewhat strayed Utopian fellowship of believers, intrepid, embattled, and unyielding, working and fighting with every means within their reach to transsubstantiate the image of the things they hope for into the actualities they live with, to transvalue the faith which is the evidence of their things unseen into the visible events and tangible facts of everyday existence. Be the outcome of their struggle what it may, it presently discloses an ethos of valor and devotion which seems to me a moving testimony to what is most hopefully human in mankind's struggle for its own humanity.[54]

vi

It was contended at the outset that Kallen applied his pluralistic allegiances, without distinction, to both ethnic and vocational concerns. In a 1942 essay, entitled "The National Being and the Jewish Community," he sees the American way of life as evoking a multipronged discipline:

The discipline . . . operates in the political order as equal suffrage; . . . in the economic order as free enterprise; in religion as freedom of conscience; in the arts and sciences as freedom of inquiry, research and expression; in education as the free public school from kindergarten to the university; and throughout these domains of the common life in freedom of association into sects, parties, corporations, trade unions, fraternal orders and whatever other groupings individual Americans choose to come together. . . . But occupational groups . . . also develop and maintain the characteristic differentiae which identify them as a group—in the Middle Ages they were often called Nations—and which constitute the culture of that group. . . .

Now the national being rests upon the cooperative and competitive relationships of these voluntary associations and consists in the free trade of goods and services between them. Their connecting links are their members. . . . This mobility of relationships is what gives its characteristic quality to the national being. Of this quality the consummation is Cultural Pluralism. For its diverse and ever-diversifying members are united with one another in and through their difference, and the singularity of our culture is the orchestration of these manifold differences—*e pluribus unum*—into the common faith which makes Liberty the foundation of Union, Union the guarantee of Liberty, and Democracy the fusion of the two in the common way of life.[55]

Kallen's welding of the ethnic and the vocational emerges in a quite unexpected setting. In the course of a visit to the Soviet Union during its early Bolshevik phase, he discovered some limited but very serious efforts at developing Jewish agrarian settlements:

The focus of this area of concentration is southern Ukraine, in the region of Kherson. In the Ukraine are collected the mass of the Jewry of Russia. In the Ukraine their sufferings had been greatest and most radical and their needs most urgent. In the Ukraine the quantity of unappropriated lands available is greater. In the Ukraine the first important experiment in the transformation of the Jew from a trader into a farmer was made. . . . The homeland of Israel, say the Russian Jewish Communists, is where collective Israel can hold land and build itself homes. . . .[56]

The tribulations of the Soviet Jewish farmer under a repressive regime are not of concern here. What is of relevance is Kallen's endorsement of a type of human association—allowing scope for corporate self-expression within a vocational context—a fellowship wherein human creative expression does lie.

Even more to the point, the convergence of Kallen's vocational, pedagogical pragmatism, and ethnic preoccupations becomes apparent in his policy projections for Palestine/Israel:

. . . Much of the misunderstanding between classes of society, not merely between rich and poor, but between carpenters and machinists, bricklayers and plumbers, farmers and industrialists, physicians and mechanics, is due to their failure imaginatively to realize each others' lives. This failure comes from the absence of common fundamental experience in the business of living. A man who has never actually spread dung in a wheatfield, cleared out an irrigation ditch, run a lathe, or mended a road can never get the outlook of one whose life consists in doing just that and nothing more. There are, undoubtedly, in every population, a proportion of persons whose abilities extend to nothing more. And it is recognized that there are also a far greater proportion known as "the average man" who can live and work on a richer and more varied level, but who do not get the opportunity. It is agreed, moreover, that no educational system is competent which does not supply the maximum of opportunity. . . . But it still remains inexorably a fact that every community rests upon certain basic activities—the so-called "dirty work" of civilized society—In this "dirty work," hence, every citizen should have a share: The time for this work is during the school age—in the vacations of the period from the fourteenth to the twentieth year. . . .
    Education would thus be made to play its inevitable role to the advantage and not the obstruction of the development of the Jewish homeland. Take care of education, says Plato, and education will take care of everything else. . . . In the end the success or failure of the New Zion will be attributable to the quality, extent, direction, and competency of its educational system.[57]

The vocation of soldiering blends inseparably with the education of Israel's polyglot citizenry. Kallen contrasts the Israeli attitude with that prevailing in the United States:

As over the generations I had been pointing out to my pupils in the philosophy of education, among our democracies the function of the soldier had been divorced from the function of the citizen; war, so personal in every people's history, had been denied a role in the training for citizenship in a free society of free men. . . . All machines, all tools and

engines of peace and war, can be only so much junk without the mind and
heart of the worker and fighter who puts them to use . . . and school and
army had somehow to be meshed together in one continuous educational
endeavor whose consummation should be that adam hadash [new man],
that new Israeli, of whom, the old hope possessed no image.[58]

To the military, through compulsory service, was to be assigned the
paramount mission of Israelizing the diverse youth population—along pluralistic lines—eschewing a "melting pot" model. The goal was to help develop

. . . the more than half a million of the newly Ingathered from sixty
countries and seventy-four divergent cultures, with their different languages and their often incommensurable folkways and mores, as the adam
hadash with a common speech, a common loyalty, and a shared understanding of himself as a citizen of Israel, of Israel as a nation among the
nations, and of mankind in the universe that science discloses and history,
Jewish history interprets.[59]

The anticipated outcome of this unifying experience was not to be a totalistic
commitment. Rather, the emergent insight was to be a belief that

the cultures of mankind are indefeasibly plural and that human beings are
freest and happiest and most originative when the cultures they live in
freely orchestrate to one another in an ever-diversifying teamplay of their
differences.[60]

Several of the early architects of the American nation, in projecting their
vision of its future development, expressed their aspirations in terms of a
New Zion. Horace Kallen, deeply imbued as he was with the grandeur of
America's ideals, transferred some of his ardor and attachments to Zion. In
that Old/New Land, factitious distinctions between "culture" and "vocation,"
between humanistic education and education for national survival would
vanish. As he declared in one of his final writings:

The discipline of freedom is a form of "togetherness." . . . It builds on the
steady purpose to find how in any endeavor of the mind, the hand or the
heart or of all three jointly, people who are different from each other can act
together with each other, and each fulfill his self-hood more abundantly
than he could by going it alone.[61]

Notes

1. Spencer J. Maxcy, "Horace Kallen's Two Conceptions of Cultural Pluralism,"
Educational Theory 29 (Winter 1979).
    2. Ibid., p. 38.
    3. Horace M. Kallen, *William James and Henri Bergson* (Chicago, 1914), pp. 104–5.

4. Ibid., p. 182.

5. Horace M. Kallen, ed., *The Philosophy of William James* (New York, 1925), p. 7.

6. Ibid., pp. 37–38.

7. Kallen, *James and Bergson*, pp. 144–45, 152–53.

8. Horace M. Kallen, *Ideals and Experience* (Ithaca, N.Y., 1948), pp. 52–53. See also Kallen's musings on the "absolute pragmatism" of his admired but rejected teacher, Josiah Royce: "Remarks on Royce's Philosophy," *The Journal of Philosophy* 53 (2 February 1956).

9. Horace M. Kallen, *Creativity, Imagination, Logic* (New York, 1973), p. 208.

10. Horace M. Kallen, *Secularism Is The Will of God* (New York, 1954), p. 100.

11. Ibid., p. 104.

12. Kallen, *Creativity*, p. 121.

13. Horace M. Kallen, *The Book of Job as a Greek Tragedy* (New York, 1959), pp. 45–46.

14. Kallen, *Secularism*, p. 11.

15. Kallen, *Creativity*, p. 142.

16. Horace M. Kallen, *Art and Freedom* (1942; reprint, Westport Conn., 1969), 2:932–33.

17. Horace M. Kallen, *Art and Freedom* (New York, 1942), 1:xvi. See also Kallen's deploring of Soviet censorship applied to the journal of humor, *Krokodil:* "The Comic Spirit in the Freedom of Man," *Teachers College Record* 48 (December 1966): 194.

18. Horace M. Kallen, *Frontiers of Hope* (1929; reprint, New York, 1977) pp. 139–40.

19. Quoted in Horace M. Kallen, *Utopians at Bay* (New York, 1958), p. 246.

20. Josiah Royce, "The Nature of Community," in Max H. Fisch, ed., *Classic American Philosophers* (New York, 1951), p. 209.

21. Horace M. Kallen, *Modernity and Liberty* (Buffalo, N.Y., 1947), pp. 121–22. For the distinction between "orchestration" and "integration," see Horace M. Kallen, *What I Believe and Why—Maybe* (New York, 1971), pp. 196–97.

22. Horace M. Kallen, *A Free Society* (New York, 1934), pp. 33–34.

23. Ibid., pp. 37–38.

24. Kallen, *Creativity*, p. 190.

25. Horace M. Kallen, *"Of Them Which Say They are Jews"—and Other Essays on the Jewish Struggle for Survival* (New York, 1954), pp. 81–84.

26. Maxcy, "Kallen's Two Conceptions," p. 33. For a penetrating analysis (with which the present writer entertains some disagreements) of Deweyan and Jamesian views on individuality and the social group, see Jay Wissot, "John Dewey, Horace Meyer Kallen, and Cultural Pluralism," *Educational Theory* 25 (Spring 1975). See also a response by Seymour W. Itzkoff, "The Sources of Culture Pluralism," *Educational Theory* 26(Spring 1976).

27. Horace M. Kallen, *Zionism and World Politics: A Study in History and Social Psychology* (1921; reprint, Westport Conn., 1975), p. 138.

28. Horace M. Kallen, *Cultural Pluralism and the American Idea* (Philadelphia, 1956), pp. 180–81.

29. Ibid., p. 45.

30. Ibid., p. 52.

31. Kallen, *"Of Them Which Say,"* p. 58 n.1.

32. Ibid., pp. 83–84.

33. Kallen, *Cultural Pluralism*, p. 98.

34. Horace M. Kallen, *Judaism at Bay* (New York, 1932), p. 79.

35. Ibid., pp. 84, 83.

36. Horace M. Kallen, a 1933 speech reprinted by Arthur Hertzberg, *The Zionist Idea* (New York, 1960), p. 531.

37. Kallen, *Judaism at Bay*, pp. 38–39.

38. Kallen, speech reprinted by Hertzberg, *Zionist Idea*, pp. 532–33.

39. Maxcy, "Kallen's Two Conceptions," p. 31.

40. Kallen, *Zionism*, pp. 136, 142–45.

41. Kallen, *"Of Them Which Say,"* pp. 55–57. See also Horace M. Kallen, "Cultural Pluralism and the Jews," *Jewish Spectator* 42 (Fall 1977). Originally delivered as an address, 7 December 1972.

42. Ibid., pp. 28–29.

43. Ibid., pp. 85–86.

44. Kallen, *Judaism at Bay*, p. 38.

45. Abdelwahab M. Elmessiri, *The Land of Promise* (New Brunswick, N.J., 1977), p. 15.

46. Kallen, *"Of Them Which Say,"* p. 190.

47. Ibid., p. 98.

48. Kallen, *Judaism at Bay*, pp. 40–41.

49. Kallen, *"Of Them Which Say,"* pp. 70–71.

50. Ibid., p. 70.

51. Ibid., pp. 93–94.

52. Ibid., p. 98.

53. Ibid., pp. 95, 97.

54. Kallen, *Utopians*, p. 290.

55. Kallen, *"Of Them Which Say,"* pp. 81–84.

56. Kallen, *Frontiers*, p. 396.

57. Kallen, *Zionism*, pp. 329–31. See also Horace M. Kallen, "The American Worker and His Education," *Social Research* 11 (February 1944).

58. Kallen, *Utopians*, p. 218.

59. Ibid., p. 218.

60. Ibid., p. 245.

61. Kallen, *What I Believe*, p. 203.

Notes on Contributors

Lewis S. Feuer, University Professor of Sociology and Government, Emeritus, University of Virginia; author of *Einstein and the Generations of Science; The Scientific Intellectual; Spinoza and the Rise of Liberalism*, and other works.

Milton R. Konvitz, Professor of Industrial and Labor Relations, and Professor of Law, Emeritus, Cornell University; author of *Judaism and the American Idea; Religious Liberty and Conscience; Expanding Liberties;* coeditor of *Jewish Social Studies;* editor (with Sidney Hook) of *Freedom and Experience: Essays Presented to H. M. Kallen.*

Ronald Kronish, Director of Staff Development for Centers for Jewish-Zionist Education, Jerusalem; Lecturer in Education, Tel Aviv University.

Elmer N. Lear, Professor of Social Science, Emeritus, Pennsylvania State University.

Sidney Ratner, Professor of History, Emeritus, Rutgers University; author of books and articles on American economic and intellectual history; editor, *Vision and Action: Essays in Honor of H. M. Kallen.*

Sarah Schmidt, Director of Rockland Community College Program in Israel, Jerusalem; formerly on faculty of University of Maryland; author of numerous articles on Horace Kallen's role in the history of American Zionism.

BIO KAL